COMBAT
The Great American Warplanes

Popular
Mechanics

COMBAT
The Great American Warplanes

By Jim Wilson

Hearst Books

ISBN 1-58816-064-5
Library of Congress Cataloging-in-Publication Data
POPULAR MECHANICS Combat/by the Editors of POPULAR MECHANICS.
p. cm.
1. Airplanes, Military. I. POPULAR MECHANICS.

UG1240 .P67 2001
623.7'46—dc21   2001016929

COMBAT: The Great American Warplanes
Editorial Director: Morin Bishop
  Project Editor: Andrew Blais
  Designers: Vincent Mejia, Barbara Chilenskas
  Senior Editor: John Bolster
  Photography Editor: John Blackmar
  Managing Editor: Theresa M. Deal
  Copy Editor: A. Lee Fjordbotten
  Reporters: Kate Brash, Ward Calhoun

COMBAT was prepared by
Bishop Books
611 Broadway
New York, NY 10012

First Edition
10 9 8 7 6 5 4 3 2 1
Printed in China

www.popularmechanics.com

Contents

Chapter 1: Fighters Learn to Fly   **6**

Chapter 2: Bombers   **12**
Overview 14 / Boeing B-17 Flying Fortress 20 / Boeing B-29 Superfortress 24
Convair B-36 Peacemaker 26 / Boeing B-52 Stratofortress 28
Northrop B-2 Spirit 32

Chapter 3: Fighters   **36**
Overview 38 / SPAD XIII 44 / Lockheed P-38 Lightning 48
Curtiss P-40 Warhawk 52 / Republic P-47 Thunderbolt 54
North American P-51 Mustang 56 / Lockheed P-80 Shooting Star 60
North American P-86 Sabre 62 / McDonnell F-4 Phantom II 64
McDonnell F-15 Eagle 66 / General Dynamics F-16 Fighting Falcon 68
Lockheed F-117 Nighthawk 72

Chapter 4: Attack Aircraft   **74**
Overview 76 / Douglas A-20 Havoc 82 / Vought A-7 Corsair II 84
Fairchild A-10 Thunderbolt 86 / McDonnell Douglas AV-8B Harrier II 92

Chapter 5: Reconnaissance and Electronic-Warfare Planes   **94**
Overview 96 / Lockheed U-2 Dragon Lady 102 / Lockheed SR-71
Blackbird 104 / Boeing E-3 Sentry 108 / Boeing E-4 NAOC 110

Chapter 6: Cargo, Transports and Tankers   **114**
Overview 116 / Douglas C-47 Skytrain 122 / Waco CG-4A Haig 126
McDonnell Douglas KC-10 Extender 128

Chapter 7: Helicopters   **130**
Overview 132 / Bell H-13 Sioux 138 / Boeing CH-47 Chinook 140
Bell AH-1 Cobra 142 / Sikorsky UH-60 Black Hawk 146
McDonnell Douglas AH-64 Apache 148 / Boeing-Sikorsky RAH-66 Comanche 152

Chapter 8: Wings of the Navy   **154**
Overview 156 / Consolidated PBY Catalina 162 / Vought F4U Corsair 166
Curtiss SB2C Helldiver 168 / Boeing CH-46 Sea Knight 172
USS Abraham Lincoln CVN-72 174 / Grumman A-6 Intruder 176
Grumman F-14 Tomcat 178 / McDonnell Douglas F/A-18 Hornet 182

Chapter 9: The Future and Experimental   **186**

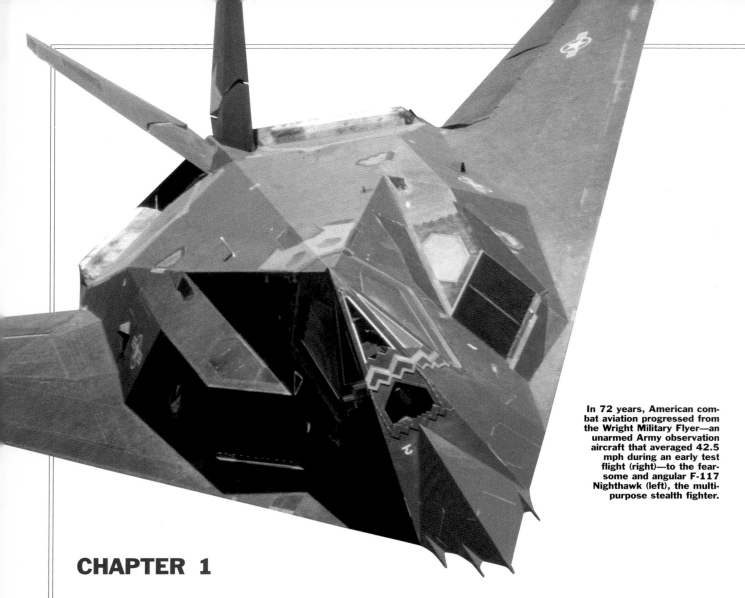

In 72 years, American combat aviation progressed from the Wright Military Flyer—an unarmed Army observation aircraft that averaged 42.5 mph during an early test flight (right)—to the fearsome and angular F-117 Nighthawk (left), the multipurpose stealth fighter.

CHAPTER 1

Fighters Learn to Fly

The U.S. Department of War did not beat a path to the Wright Brothers' door after the revelations at Kitty Hawk. Getting military forces airborne proved to be a steep climb in more ways than one.

In the early hours of January 17, 1991, a pair of United States Air Force F-117 Nighthawks penetrated the Iraqi sky. Painted night-black and cloaked with radar-deflecting stealth technology, the jets cruised, unchallenged, toward downtown Baghdad; moments later, the AT&T Communications Center collapsed beneath the assault of a laser-guided bomb while the buildings around it remained unscathed. Video footage of such precision munitions—a crosshair-framed missile streak-

ing into an exploding target—became a central icon of the Gulf War, furnishing a powerful reminder of one of the greatest technological developments of the 20th century: the emergence of the modern combat plane.

Popular histories of air power create the impression that after the Wright Brothers' famous flight on December 17, 1903, the American military championed combat aircraft, but the story follows a more convoluted path. For decades, the War

Department took aggressive steps to *discourage* flight. The U.S. Army delayed buying a Wright Brothers plane until President Theodore Roosevelt ordered the purchase of a 1909 Wright Military Flyer. Almost immediately, the plane and its partially trained pilots were hustled off to distant Fort Sam Houston in San Antonio, Texas, assigned to the unglamorous Signal Corps and supplied with a paltry budget of $2.88 a week for fuel, oil and repairs. Even after aircraft had proven themselves in World War I, the government hesitated. As late as 1925 the President's Aircraft Board warned: "The next war may well start in the air but in all probability will wind up, as the last war did, in the mud." The War Department, however, had good

reason to be skeptical. Only nine days before the Wright Brothers took off from Kitty Hawk, the Army had concluded its own aviation experiments with the spectacular crash of the Great Aerodrome.

The Great Aerodrome, the U.S. Army's forgotten airplane, was a flimsy, 55-ft.-long, propeller-driven creation of Samuel Pierpont Langley, arguably 19th-century America's most politically connected scientist. When he was in his early 50s, Langley, a highly regarded solar astronomer, had become fascinated with flight. After spending several years collecting data on lift, thrust and other flight characteristics, he began building a series of model aircraft, which he called "aerodromes." His tandem-winged miniatures resembled stubby dragon-

The Great Aerodrome (above), locked in place at the end of a catapult track atop a houseboat on the Potomac River, provided shade under its nearly 50-ft. wingspan for a group of nonplussed workers prior to one of its dramatic crashes. Two successful flights of a quarter-scale model in June 1901 and August 1903 belied the aerodynamic problems inherent in the full-size aircraft.

After repairs, Langley's Great Aerodrome was ready to catch its "second wind" in December 1903 (above, left). Upon launching, however (above, right), it plummeted straight down, snapped in two and landed upside down in the Potomac—hitting the water, according to a Washington reporter, "like a handful of mortar." The Army's interest in aviation was duly curbed for much of the decade.

flies and took off via catapult from the top of a houseboat, remaining aloft thanks to propellers driven by steam engines. By the spring of 1896, the 20-pound gasoline-powered version could fly nearly a mile. The tests convinced Langley that manned flight in a heavier-than-air flying machine was simply a matter of scaling up his Aerodrome and building a catapult powerful enough to launch it. At a time when a locomotive cost $20,000, Langley estimated his single-seat Aerodrome would cost $50,000—a huge sum by most accounts, but not for the coffers of Langley's primary patron: the United States Government.

As secretary of the Smithsonian Institution, Langley was, in effect, one of the government's chief scientists. When he spoke, influential men listened, and for the next two years the Great Aerodrome was his favorite topic of conversation. In 1898, on the eve of the Spanish-American War, the seeds Langley had so assiduously sown finally sprouted: At the suggestion of President William McKinley, the War Department Board of Ordnance and Fortification awarded Langley a $50,000 grant to build the Great Aerodrome.

Before long, the project took on the worst

characteristics of a modern-day defense contract. It fell years behind schedule and climbed nearly 50 percent over budget. Finally, on October 7, 1903—five years after work had begun—the Great Aerodrome was ready to fly. Now nearly 70, Langley designated Charles M. Manly, his assistant who had retooled the plane's engine, as test pilot. The project's secrecy—Langley refused local newspaper interviews—heightened the curiosity of the crowds that gathered along the shore of the Potomac River, near Widewater, Virginia, to watch the flight. After several tension-building delays, Manly climbed to the roof of the houseboat, started the engine and settled into the crude cockpit. When the propellers buzzed to full speed, the catapult fired. A reporter for POPULAR MECHANICS described what happened next:

"It went down from its 60-foot height about as rapidly as would a cannon ball hurled with the same force, and on striking the water began its wonderful diving performance that proclaims it a splendid success as a submarine. A shout of joy went up when [Manly's] head showed above the waves."

Langley ordered the Great Aerodrome repaired, and on December 8 the intrepid Manly was ready

The Liberty Plane (above) was the American-built version of the British de Havilland DH-4 bomber. After initial problems with its new 400-hp V12 engine were resolved, the DH-4 was capable of speeds up to 124 mph, enabling it to match or outrun most fighters of the World War I era. The B-2 Spirit (right) cut a striking, ominous figure as it cruised over a California desert landscape in July 1989.

to fly again. This time the fragile Aerodrome reared up and began to collapse into itself the moment the catapult fired. Manly again plunged with the wreckage into the frigid Potomac and was momentarily trapped under the water, surviving, although badly chilled. When Langley approached the government for money to attempt a third test, the War Department refused, and the Army, under threat of congressional investigations, quietly withdrew their interest in mastery of the skies. The War Department's conservatism toward aviation led the United States to enter World War I without a single operational combat aircraft—U.S. aces would earn their honors flying planes of foreign design.

In the years that followed the Great War, the Army, Navy and Marines independently recognized the importance of aviation. World War II clarified the need for an additional armed service, the United States Air Force. This is the story of the evolution of American air power through the

aircraft that made it possible. While it is undoubtedly true that many nations played important roles in the development of aircraft, especially in the pre-World War I era, the story of combat aviation is chiefly an American tale. *Combat* focuses on 40 aircraft that represent pivotal points in the evolution of modern combat planes. Given the scope of American military aviation, any such "best of" list is inevitably somewhat arbitrary and will probably omit one or two reader favorites. But we have endeavored to be as comprehensive as possible within the confines of our format, exploring the major families of combat planes: bombers, fighters, attack planes, transports and tankers, reconnaissance and electronic-warfare planes, and helicopters. In addition, *Combat* describes how these aircraft were adapted to operate at sea and takes a look onboard a modern aircraft carrier. The story of U.S. combat aviation closes with a look at experimental military aircraft—the potential great American warplanes of the future.

B-29 Superfortresses, 1945

CHAPTER 2
Bombers

An XB-47 (left) prototype performed a takeoff test with a little help from 18 aft-mounted 1000-pound-thrust rockets, at Moses Lake Air Force Base in Washington state in 1948. B-47s were the first swept-wing mass-produced jet bombers and stalwarts of medium-range bombing in the 1950s. An airman (above) peered from the forward bombing and sighting station of a B-17G Flying Fortress.

Bombers

Perhaps the most important type of aircraft in America's flight arsenal during World War II and the ensuing Cold War, the bomber greatly extended the reach of an infant superpower.

At the beginning of the 20th century, the Great White Fleet embodied America's ability to project its influence abroad. The sight of those majestic battleships glistening in the waters off foreign shores announced that the United States had become the military equal to the great nations of Europe. As the century closed, America remained the only true superpower due in part to the strategic prowess made possible by a new kind of aircraft: the bomber.

The value of a specialized aircraft that could drop explosives behind enemy lines on munitions plants, fuel depots and other industrial centers was quickly revealed during World War I. Initially,

A North African-based Consolidated B-24 Liberator skimmed the smokestacks of Ploesti, Romania, during an American attack on the city's oil fields on August 1, 1943.

A Martin B-26B (above), which functioned as a medium-range bomber during World War II, sat on the runway in Algeria in 1942, its crew gathered in front of the nose. The B-26B had several flaws, such as a long takeoff run and fast landing speeds, which mandated significant alterations to subsequent models and earned the plane an unwanted nickname, the "Widow Maker."

advocates of military aviation had believed that bombing front-line positions would break the siege of trench warfare. Early attempts to release explosives at low altitudes failed miserably however; the poorly aimed explosives tumbled out of control through the air and ricocheted away from their targets. Dropping bombs from higher altitudes gave bombardiers much more time to aim, thereby improving accuracy but lengthening the time a slow-moving aircraft remained exposed to deadly ground fire from the trenches.

In fact, development of higher-altitude bombers had begun well before the Great War. In July 1913, less than 10 years after the Wright Brothers' historic flight, Igor Sikorsky, the father of the helicopter, flew the first true heavy bomber, the Il'ya Muromets (IM). Powered by four English-built engines, the IM-class aircraft—which could take much more abuse than their single- and double-engine relatives—would give Russia the world's first strategic bombing force. Each of the bi-winged aircraft carried 2200 pounds of bombs and protected its six-man crew with a fully enclosed flight deck. Some 80 IM-class bombers fought against the Germans until the Bolshevik Revolution ended Russia's involvement in the war. As the fighting dragged on, England, France, Germany and Italy successfully developed heavy bombers of their own. After the armistice, however, combat-aviation development was greatly slowed. Treaty limitations forestalled

German activity, and war weariness among the victors caused military budgets to shrink. The American military remained unconvinced of the airplane's military potential, and a War Department evaluation concluded in 1919, "Nothing so far brought out in the war shows that aerial activities can be carried on, independently of ground forces, to such an extent as to affect materially the conduct of the war as a whole."

The solution to the bombing dilemma emerged from a seemingly unlikely event: demobilization. By the end of World War I, 20,000 officers and 178,000 enlisted men filled the ranks of the Army Air Service. A year after Armistice Day, however, only one officer in 10 and one enlisted man in 20 remained. Many who left would form the nucleus of a new American industry—commercial aviation. In the course of designing and building better commercial airplanes, these Air Service veterans developed engines with superchargers and turbochargers, raising the ceiling at which air-

craft could operate and allowing strategic bombers to fly high enough to avoid enemy ground fire.

In America, bombers were envisioned as weapons for sinking enemy fleets before they brought their big guns in range of American ports. In 1931, a long-running dispute between the U.S. Army and U.S. Navy ended with an agreement that gave the Army Air Corps responsibility for coastal defense. With this mission in mind, the Boeing Aircraft Company adapted one of its commercial airliner designs to create a new, multi-engine bomber, the B-17 Flying Fortress. When Hitler's tanks rumbled across Poland in 1939, America's heavy-bomber force consisted of only 23 B-17s, but with the infrastructure of the commercial airline industry in place, the nation was equipped to mass produce thousands more as trouble brewed in Europe. By the end of World War II, more than 12,000 B-17s had taken to the sky.

Although the speed, range, armament and payload capability of the B-17 improved steadily over

The paint job on the ordnance-laden Martin B-57B Canberra above stood out in the daylight but camouflaged the plane during night missions. The versatile B-57 served the USAF from 1954 to '79, acting as a bomber, nuclear-weapons platform, spyplane, tow target, weather-observation plane and electronic-countermeasure aircraft. B-57s delivered to Pakistan saw action in the 1965 Kashmir conflict.

The B-1B (above), which was revived by President Reagan in 1982, tested in 1984 and deployed in October 1986, is a long-range heavy bomber capable of flying across oceans before refueling. The aircraft has a wingspan of 137 ft., a ceiling of 60,000 ft. and a crew of four, consisting of an aircraft commander, a pilot, an offensive-systems operator and a defensive-systems operator.

its production cycle, its roots as a coastal-defense aircraft limited it to the distances encountered in the European theater. Japan's presence in the war, however, created the need for a revolutionary new type of plane, the extended-range heavy bomber. The first effort to produce such an aircraft, the Boeing B-29 Superfortress, represented the next evolutionary step in bomber design. It also figured prominently in an action that changed the very nature of warfare: In August 1945, two specially modified B-29s dropped primitive nuclear bombs on Hiroshima and Nagasaki, ending World War II and redefining strategic bombing.

The ancient tradition of distinguishing combatants and civilians, previously blurred when Dresden and Tokyo were leveled by fire-bombing cam-

paigns, had been completely obliterated. When Russia, an ally in World War II, became America's Cold War enemy, the next generation of U.S. strategic bombers was built. Forming a linchpin in the doctrine of Mutual Assured Destruction, a series of increasingly larger and longer-range aircraft—based on the U.S. mainland and capable of striking Soviet targets on the other side of the globe—culminated in the giant Boeing B-52 Stratofortress and, later, the stealthy Northrop B-2 Spirit.

With the B-2, the technology for projecting America's will abroad had run the spectrum, from the most visible symbol of power, the battleship and its high-profile accompanying fleet, to the most subtle, a nearly invisible bomber with the capability of destroying an entire city.

With smoke from the burning factory visible in the background, a Boeing B-17F Flying Fortress (above) flew to safety in October 1943 after participating In a daylight raid that targeted the Focke-Wulf Plant in Marienburg, Germany, from 13,000 ft.; the deep-penetration precision raid made a considerable dent in production of Fw-190 fighters for the Luftwaffe.

B-17
Flying Fortress
• Boeing

With its fearsome defensive array of .30- and .50-cal. machine guns, the B-17 was ubiquitous in the wartime skies over Europe.

Conceived in 1934, the Boeing B-17 Flying Fortress was more than a weapon—it was also a statement of faith. In the years after World War I, America had turned isolationist, and military budgets were cut to reflect its reticence about foreign entanglements. Yet, there remained Army officers and aircraft builders who believed that a strategic bombing force was essential to the nation's future defense. Investing over a quarter-million dollars of its own money during the depths of the Great Depression—in effect betting the future of the company—Boeing Aircraft responded to the Army's requirement for a 200-mph aircraft, capable of delivering 2000 pounds of bombs, with an imag-

VITALS

Designation	B-17G Flying Fortress
Wingspan	103 ft. 9 in.
Length	74 ft. 9 in.
Gross Weight	65,000 pounds
Top Speed	302 mph
Cruising Speed	160 mph
Range	3400 miles
Ceiling	35,600 ft.

inative design that was both radical and familiar.

At first glance, the most striking feature of the low-wing, four-engine plane, which originally flew as the Boeing Model 299 on July 28, 1935, was that it bristled with defensive armaments, including five .30-cal. machine guns mounted in transparent bubbles called "blisters." Awed by this array of unprecedented firepower, *Seattle Times* journalist Richard L. Williams described the prototype as a "15-ton Flying Fortress." The nickname stuck.

From the perspective of the aviation expert, the most impressive feature of the Flying Fortress was not its armaments but the basic familiarity of its airframe. Boeing was in the business of making commercial as well as military aircraft, and a Flying Fortress stripped of its armaments and two of its engines bore a striking resemblance to the Boeing 247, one of the company's commercial-airliner models.

For a pilot, the most obvious improvement seen in the B-17 was its fully enclosed flight deck. Previously, Boeing military aircraft had open cockpits, which pilots tended to prefer due to the clear line of sight it afforded them, but as planes flew higher and faster, this feature of World War I-era aircraft began to impede performance. Enclosing the pilot, copilot, bombardier, radio operator and five gunners streamlined the aircraft, improved the plane's speed and raised its operational ceiling. Four 1200-hp Wright R-1820 Cyclone engines gave the B-17 the turbocharged strength to outrun most fighters.

Flying Fortresses first went to war in 1941 when the War Department sent 20 of the 323-mph B-17C versions to the British Royal Air Force. The pilots and flight crews hated them, a response that fueled the B-17's evolution. Boeing answered the critics by beefing up the armor and adding self-sealing fuel tanks. By the time the Japanese attacked Pearl Harbor, the B-17E packed nine machine guns, sported a redesigned tail—adding nearly 6 ft. to the plane's body—and introduced remote-controlled turrets in the belly and dorsal fuselage.

Throughout the war, the plane continued to evolve. The most advanced model, the B-17G, defended itself with 12 .50-cal. machine guns, hefted 8000 pounds of bombs and had a ceiling of 35,600 ft., the cruising altitude of a modern Boeing 737. Boeing would eventually build 6981 B-17s. Under a cooperative arrangement, Douglas and Lockheed would build 5750 more.

Flying Fortresses drew first blood in the Pacific three days after Pearl Harbor, when a B-17 based in the Philippines sank the heavy cruiser *Ashigara*.
(continued)

A B-17G (above) cruised over mountainous Southern California in 1943 before heading to the European Theater of Operations, where the missions were more suited to the range of the Flying Fortress than those of the Pacific Theater.

Although initially stationed around the globe, virtually all of the existing B-17s at the time, and most subsequent versions, would eventually see combat over the skies of Europe. The summer after the U.S. entered the war, B-17s began hammering targets in France and, later, Germany.

By the end of the war, Flying Fortresses had dropped more bombs than any American aircraft. The tightly knit flight crews who flew B-17s suffered enormous losses—some 4750 planes were downed, and thousands more limped home with missing engines, fragmented fuselages and gaping holes in wings. General Henry H. "Hap" Arnold, the commander of the U.S. Army Air Forces during the Second World War, aptly described them as the "backbone of our worldwide aerial offensive."

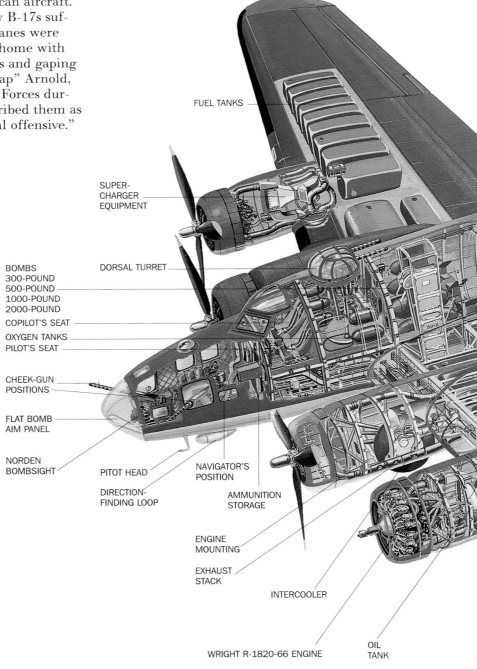

FUEL TANKS

SUPER-
CHARGER
EQUIPMENT

BOMBS
300-POUND
500-POUND
1000-POUND
2000-POUND

DORSAL TURRET

COPILOT'S SEAT

OXYGEN TANKS

PILOT'S SEAT

CHEEK-GUN
POSITIONS

FLAT BOMB
AIM PANEL

NORDEN
BOMBSIGHT

PITOT HEAD

DIRECTION-
FINDING LOOP

NAVIGATOR'S
POSITION

AMMUNITION
STORAGE

ENGINE
MOUNTING

EXHAUST
STACK

INTERCOOLER

WRIGHT R-1820-66 ENGINE

OIL
TANK

B-17F Flying Fortress

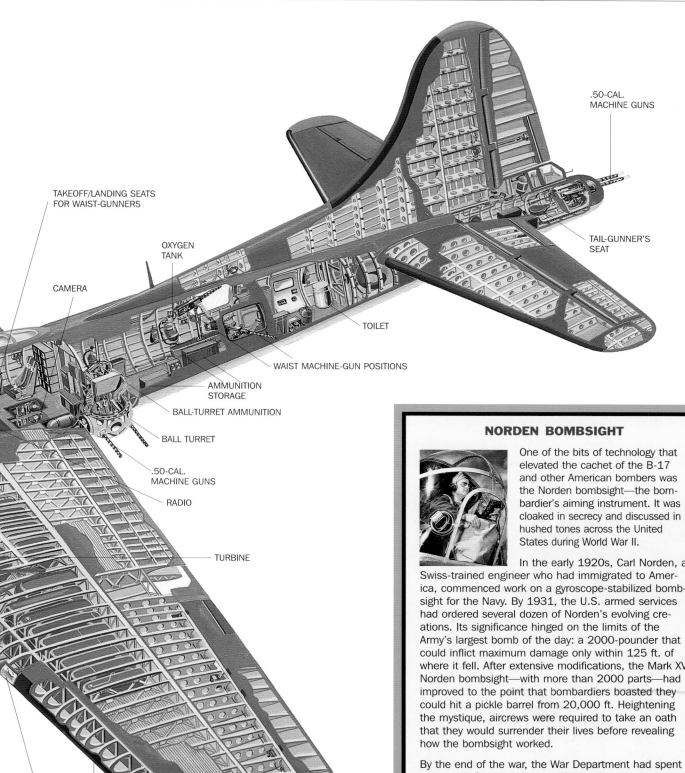

.50-CAL.
MACHINE GUNS

TAKEOFF/LANDING SEATS
FOR WAIST-GUNNERS

TAIL-GUNNER'S
SEAT

OXYGEN
TANK

CAMERA

TOILET

WAIST MACHINE-GUN POSITIONS

AMMUNITION
STORAGE

BALL-TURRET AMMUNITION

BALL TURRET

.50-CAL.
MACHINE GUNS

RADIO

TURBINE

DE-ICING BOOT

LANDING LIGHT

NORDEN BOMBSIGHT

One of the bits of technology that elevated the cachet of the B-17 and other American bombers was the Norden bombsight—the bombardier's aiming instrument. It was cloaked in secrecy and discussed in hushed tones across the United States during World War II.

In the early 1920s, Carl Norden, a Swiss-trained engineer who had immigrated to America, commenced work on a gyroscope-stabilized bombsight for the Navy. By 1931, the U.S. armed services had ordered several dozen of Norden's evolving creations. Its significance hinged on the limits of the Army's largest bomb of the day: a 2000-pounder that could inflict maximum damage only within 125 ft. of where it fell. After extensive modifications, the Mark XV Norden bombsight—with more than 2000 parts—had improved to the point that bombardiers boasted they could hit a pickle barrel from 20,000 ft. Heightening the mystique, aircrews were required to take an oath that they would surrender their lives before revealing how the bombsight worked.

By the end of the war, the War Department had spent more than $1 billion for 90,000 Norden bombsights. Accurate though it may have been in tests, the variables of actual combat never allowed the Norden bombsight to live up to its "pickle barrel" reputation—less than one-third of the bombs dropped on Germany hit the ground within 1000 ft. of their targets.

Pressed into service tests in June 1943, the B-29 Superfortress (above) carried out the bombardment of Imperial Japan in mid-1945, destroying almost every strategic target in the Japanese home islands by August. The most well-known B-29 mission was that of Colonel Paul Tibbets's *Enola Gay*—the first wartime deployment of an atomic bomb, dropped on Hiroshima, August 6, 1945.

B-29
Superfortress

• Boeing

With its distinctive design features and remote-controlled gun turrets, the B-29 Superfortress was in a class all its own.

Even if the Boeing B-29 Superfortress had not dropped atomic bombs on Hiroshima and Nagasaki, it would have earned its place in history as the most technologically sophisticated bomber of World War II. The B-29 was the product of a lengthy battle within the War Department over the need for a bomber with capabilities superior to the Boeing B-17 Flying Fortress. In early 1940, the U.S. Army Air Corps ended the debate by issuing a requirement for a bomber that could carry a 2000-pound payload 5000 miles at 400 mph. Lockheed and Dou-

glas dropped out of the competition, and the War Department ordered three air-worthy prototypes from Boeing. The first, designated the XB-29, flew on September 21, 1942.

The B-29 was a true technological marvel. Its most obvious break with previous bombers was a long, narrow, almost gliderlike wing that Boeing engineers had optimized for high-speed flight. Large flaps that extended prior to takeoffs and landings created the additional lift needed for low-speed flight. The B-29's powerplant consisted of

VITALS	
Designation	B-29 Superfortress
Wingspan	141 ft. 2¾ in.
Length	99 ft.
Gross Weight	105,000 pounds
Top Speed	357 mph
Cruising Speed	220 mph
Range	5600 miles
Ceiling	33,600 ft.

four 2200-hp Wright Double-Cyclone engines.

The most revolutionary developments were inside the aircraft. Pressurized compartments let the flight crew and the rear gunner fly in relative comfort. For defense, the B-29 featured an array of remotely controlled gun turrets—on the fuselage, behind the cockpit, near the tail and behind the nose gear—that were linked together by a primitive computer and could be fired individually or in concert when grouped by a central gunner; a fifth position, the tail guns, operated independently. Additionally, radar improved firing accuracy during night attacks. The B-29's flight time to its objectives was so lengthy that scrubbing missions simply because of bad weather over the target became unacceptable. Radar again provided a solution by "seeing" through the cloud cover so that bombardiers could release their weapons with confidence.

On June 15, 1944, nearly two years after the flight of the first XB-29 prototype, the 58th Bomber Wing flew the B-29's maiden bombing mission against the Japanese homeland, from a base in China. It was the first attack on the island nation since the dramatic Doolittle raid in April 1942. The results were disappointing, but two tactical developments would rapidly improve the aircraft's effectiveness.

The first change occurred in November 1944 when the Army Air Forces began operating B-29s from the Mariana Islands chain, shortening the trip to Japan by several hundred miles. These attacks, conducted from high altitudes over a span of three months, also fell short of expectation due to the Japanese defense industry having become too decentralized to allow for concentrated bombing raids. This dilemma led to the second major change in B-29 operations: the abandonment of precision bombing, ironically the very tactic the Superfortress was

designed to execute. Maj. Gen. Curtis E. LeMay of the 21st Bomber Command issued orders on March 8, 1945, that targeted Japanese cities. As many as 1000 B-29s staged low-level night raids, dropping napalm that touched off massive firestorms, destroying large sections of Tokyo.

The most famous B-29 attack of all, however, would not be flown by a sky-darkening fleet of bombers but by a single aircraft, the *Enola Gay*. Stripped of all defensive weaponry except its tail gun and lightened by removing its armor plating, it was one of the 509th Composite Group's 15 B-29s with the so-called "Silverplate" modification, which also involved reconfiguring their weapons bays to fit the first atomic bombs. On August 6, 1945, piloted by Col. Paul W. Tibbets Jr., the *Enola Gay* dropped the bomb "Little Boy" on Hiroshima. Three days later, a B-29 named *Bockscar*, piloted by Maj. Charles W. Sweeney, dropped a second atomic bomb, "Fat Man," on Nagasaki. Within a week, Japan had surrendered and the war was over. In the months that followed, the remaining Silverplate B-29s would form the nucleus of America's first strategic bomber force, based in Roswell, New Mexico.

A Superfort (above) dropped its load of bombs during its 150th mission over Korea, in 1951. The B-29 could carry up to 20,000 pounds of ordnance.

B-36
Peacemaker

• Convair

With its powerful presence serving as the ultimate deterrent in the Cold War's early years, the mammoth Peacemaker proved to be as good as its name.

The Convair B-36 Peacemaker was the most important bomber never to see combat. The U.S. Army Air Corps conceived the idea for the bomber in the spring of 1941, in response to Hitler's tightening grip on Western Europe. Airfields in Britain were the keystone of the forward-based bombing strategy that the Army planned to execute if America found itself drawn into another European War: Formations of B-17s and Consolidated B-24 Liberators launched from these airfields would attack German factories. Deprived of arms and ammunition, the Nazi war machine would wither as Allied ground

forces assaulted Berlin from the west and Russia attacked from the east. However, by spring 1941 there was a real possibility that Germany would invade Britain and capture the strategic airfields. If this occurred, U.S. aircraft would have to attack Germany from American soil, and to do this, the Army Air Corps would need a new, long-range bomber. Consolidated Aircraft, builder of the B-24 Liberator, responded with plans for a long-range, heavy-payload bomber, the B-36 Peacemaker.

The B-36 was so huge that the largest existing bomber, the Boeing B-29 Superfortress, could fit

The B-36 Peacemaker was the largest pusher aircraft ever produced. The D model (above) sported an innovative combination of six propellers and four G.E. jet engines. Its 230-ft. wingspan was longer than Orville Wright's first powered flight at Kitty Hawk in 1903.

beneath one of its wings. To power the massive aircraft, the B-36's design borrowed an idea from Russia's World War I-era IM-class heavy bombers: rear-mounted pusher-propellers, driven by six Pratt & Whitney Wasp Major reciprocating engines. Consolidated promised the War Department that after crossing the Atlantic the B-36 could fly over German airspace at speeds too fast to be attacked by fighters and too high to be struck by anti-aircraft guns. On target, it would release 10,000 pounds of bombs then fly back to the United States. Impressed by the numbers, the Army ordered two prototypes.

Three weeks later, Japan's surprise attack on Pearl Harbor re-wrote the strategic equation. America now faced a two-front war, and the B-36 had a new mission: to attack Tokyo from bases in Hawaii. The Army ordered 100 of the new bombers, but none would see service in World War II. Construction of B-24 Liberators took priority over ramping up production of the B-36, which wouldn't even have a test flight until almost a year to the day after the bombing of Nagasaki.

Rather than kill the B-36, the end of World War II infused the bomber with new life. In 1947, the United States undertook a sweeping reorganization of the military. A new Department of Defense replaced the War Department; a new United States Air Force consolidated some but not all of the functions previously assigned to the U.S. Army Air Forces; an Air Force Tactical Air Command would fly missions that directly supported ground troops; and a Strategic Air Command would use heavy bombers to take the war to the enemy. These planes would carry a

Inside an airplane hangar (above) at Carwell Air Force Base in Fort Worth, Texas, workers assembled a B-36 Peacemaker, the long-range bomber that helped frustrate Soviet interests in Europe for much of the Cold War.

new type of weapon, the hydrogen bomb, which could release hundreds of times the destructive force of the simple fission bombs dropped on Japan by recreating, via fusion, the thermonuclear processes that take place in the sun. And the first H-bombs were truly massive weapons—so heavy, in fact, that the B-36 was the only bomber big enough to deliver them.

The Peacemaker evolved to meet the new operational requirements of the Strategic Air Command. To assist takeoffs and speed the climb to cruising altitude, engineers added a pair of General Electric J47-GE-19 gasoline-burning jet engines to the tip of each wing. The addition of the seemingly tiny jets doubled the megabomber's horsepower, and it was a clear signal that the era of the propeller-driven bomber was ending.

In a sense, the B-36 truly lived up to the name Peacemaker. Although the service life of the giant bomber spanned over a dozen Cold War years and one major conflict—the Korean War—it was, fortunately, never called upon to unleash its weapons of mass destruction.

VITALS	
Designation	B-36D Peacemaker
Wingspan	230 ft.
Length	162 ft. 1 in.
Gross Weight	357,500 pounds
Top Speed	406 mph
Cruising Speed	225 mph
Range	8800 miles
Ceiling	45,2000 ft.

The YB-52 (above), one of two B-52 prototypes, cruised over Mt. Rainier in Washington state. Quite speedy for its size, this aircraft once averaged 625 mph on a test flight from Boeing Field in Seattle, Washington, to Wright-Patterson Air Force Base in Dayton, Ohio. In recent times, B-52 Stratofortresses dropped more than 90 cruise missiles in Iraq in 1999 during four nights of Operation Desert Fox.

B-52
Stratofortress

• Boeing

The tireless workhorses of U.S. strategic bombing, a fleet of massive Stratofortresses circled the globe 24 hours a day for more than a decade.

By the end of World War II, propeller aircraft powered by reciprocating engines had reached the peak of their development; the resulting complexities created a nightmare for flight and maintenance crews. Oil leaks forced pilots to shut down engines in flight. When the bombers landed, mechanics carried in spark plugs by the bucket—the B-36 required no fewer than 366, earning its Pratt & Whitney Wasp Major engines the nickname

"corncobs." In contrast, the J47-GE-19 jet engines that effectively doubled the Peacemaker's existing 21,000 hp were relatively trouble-free, and jet technology was a natural fit for the necessities inherent in long-range strategic bombing missions.

When the U.S. Army Air Forces announced a design competition for a new second-generation strategic bomber to replace the B-36 in 1946, Boeing submitted a concept that incorporated jet engines combined with a more aerodynamic, back-swept wing. More than 50 years later, that plane, the B-52 Stratofortress, remains the backbone of America's strategic bombing capability.

The original B-52 specifications described an aircraft that performed much like a modern commercial airliner: It had to carry a 10,000-pound payload for 5000 miles while traveling at 35,000 ft. at a minimum speed of 450 mph. Boeing's straightforward design imparted a functional reliability that encouraged the military to continually upgrade individual components rather than replace the entire plane. As new threats emerged—in Vietnam and, later, as the Soviet Union improved its air defenses—the B-52 was repeatedly upgraded to meet new mission requirements. Between 1955, when the U.S. Air Force Strategic Air Command received its first production-model B-52B, and 1962, when the last and most advanced B-52H arrived at the 4135th Strategic Wing at Minot Air Force Base in North Dakota, Boeing manufactured 744 B-52s.

During its development, the B-52's original mission underwent two profound changes. The first occurred in the late 1950s, when pilots of the high-flying U-2 photo-reconnaissance plane reported near-misses by Soviet air-defense missiles.

At Elmendorf Air Force Base in Anchorage, Alaska, Staff Sgt. Steve Campbell (on ladder) and Staff Sgt. Mike Oliver secured 500-pound practice bombs in the weapons bay of a B-52 from the 917th Reserve Wing at Barksdale Air Force Base in Louisiana, in preparation for Cope Thunder, a two-week air-power exercise in Anchorage in June 1999.

At that time, strategic bombing doctrine was based on the assumption that altitude provided protection. If radar-guided missiles could attack spyplanes flying at the B-52's cruising altitude, the only solution was to fly beneath the radar, below 500 ft. The added aerodynamic stress of low-altitude flight would require some 120 structural modifications to the Stratofortress.

In June 1977, President Jimmy Carter decided against producing the B-1 Lancer and instead chose the B-52—whose prototype had first taken to the skies over 25 years earlier—as the nation's premier strategic bomber, ordering it to be modified for long-range, air-launched cruise missile capability. The B-52, originally conceived as a deep-penetration bomber, had thus evolved into a warplane its initial designers had never imagined: a standoff missile-launching platform that could attack targets without ever coming in range of hostile fighters or air defenses.

The B-52H bombers currently in operation have eight Pratt & Whitney turbofans—generating a total of 136,000 pounds of static thrust—mounted in pairs on sharply raked forward pods under the plane's giant wings. The main landing-gear units retract into wheel wells in the body. Each unit has eight main wheels in double tandem, and two

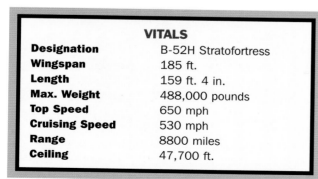

VITALS	
Designation	B-52H Stratofortress
Wingspan	185 ft.
Length	159 ft. 4 in.
Max. Weight	488,000 pounds
Top Speed	650 mph
Cruising Speed	530 mph
Range	8800 miles
Ceiling	47,700 ft.

(continued)

B-52H Stratofortress

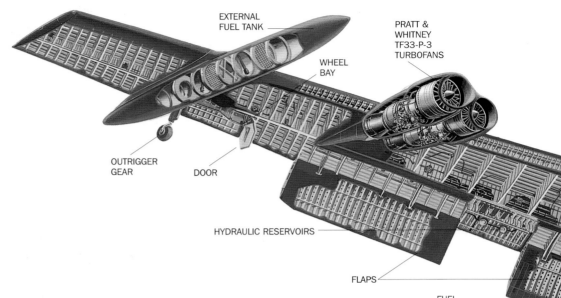

EXTERNAL FUEL TANK

PRATT & WHITNEY TF33-P-3 TURBOFANS

WHEEL BAY

OUTRIGGER GEAR

DOOR

HYDRAULIC RESERVOIRS

FLAPS

FUEL TANKS

ELECTRONIC COUNTERMEASURE ANTENNA FAIRING

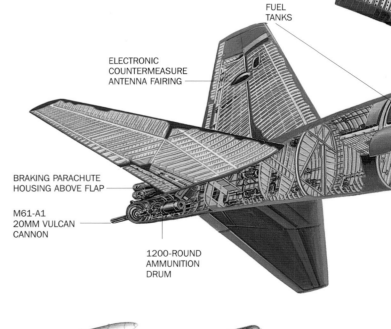

BRAKING PARACHUTE HOUSING ABOVE FLAP

M61-A1 20MM VULCAN CANNON

1200-ROUND AMMUNITION DRUM

B83 NUCLEAR

B61 NUCLEAR (TACTICAL)

MK 55 MINE

MK 60 CAPTOR MINE

MK 56 OA 05 MINE

* DOWNWARD-EJECTING SEAT

IN PM'S WORDS

New Life for Buff

"Its official name was the B-52 Stratofortress. Among aircrews its immensity and its hulking lethality soon earned it the nickname "Buff," short for Big, Ugly, Fat Fellow (or less printable variations of that theme). From the outset, it was an extraordinary airplane, worthy of its cataclysmic mission.

"The Stratofortress took up duty as America's nuclear sentinel in the mid-1950s. To avoid being caught on the ground by a surprise attack, the United States kept B-52s carrying nuclear bombs airborne above American territory 24 hours a day for more than a decade. Those flights ended in the late 1960s, but nuclear-equipped Buffs continued on alert until 1991. The bomber never had to fly the mission for which it was designed—thanks in no small measure to the fact that it could. Deterrence worked. World War III never erupted.

"Now, even though the Soviet Union self-destructed and the Cold War was won, and even though there are much newer supersonic and stealthy bombers in the fleet, the B-52 remains a vital element in the national arsenal. In fact, the Air Force is subjecting the old warriors to a variety of weapons and systems upgrades that are expected to keep the Buff a wily and formidable weapon for another 30 to 40 years or more."

—William Garvey
Popular Mechanics, March 1999

small protection wheels hang beneath the wing tips and retract into the wing after takeoff.

Without air-refueling, the B-52, carrying up to 70,000 pounds of either nuclear or conventional weapons and a crew of five, boasts a combat radius of 4300 miles. Equipped with conventional weapons, the B-52 can carry between 45 and 51 bombs on 18 to 24 external wing pylons. Another 27 fit in the bomb bay. The B-52's nuclear capac-

ity is 20 air-to-surface missiles, mounted both internally and externally.

While Stratofortresses may be chronologically older than many of the pilots who fly them, they are actually young planes. Average airtime for the fleet is about 14,000 hours. Airframe, engine and weapon modification programs undertaken over its impressive history have guaranteed that the B-52 will keep flying well into the 21st century.

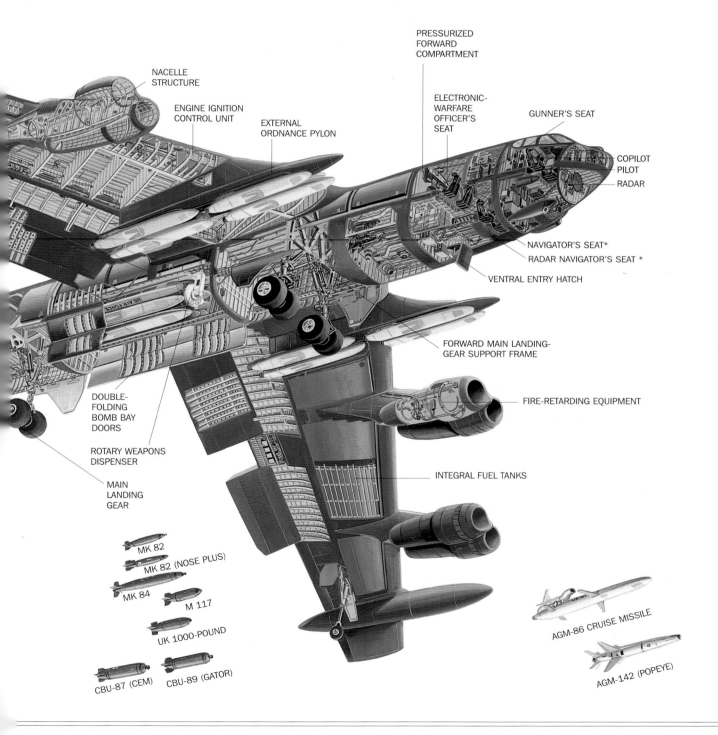

NACELLE STRUCTURE

ENGINE IGNITION CONTROL UNIT

EXTERNAL ORDNANCE PYLON

PRESSURIZED FORWARD COMPARTMENT

ELECTRONIC-WARFARE OFFICER'S SEAT

GUNNER'S SEAT

COPILOT
PILOT
RADAR

NAVIGATOR'S SEAT *
RADAR NAVIGATOR'S SEAT *
VENTRAL ENTRY HATCH

FORWARD MAIN LANDING-GEAR SUPPORT FRAME

FIRE-RETARDING EQUIPMENT

DOUBLE-FOLDING BOMB BAY DOORS

ROTARY WEAPONS DISPENSER

MAIN LANDING GEAR

INTEGRAL FUEL TANKS

MK 82
MK 82 (NOSE PLUS)
MK 84
M 117
UK 1000-POUND
CBU-87 (CEM)   CBU-89 (GATOR)

AGM-86 CRUISE MISSILE

AGM-142 (POPEYE)

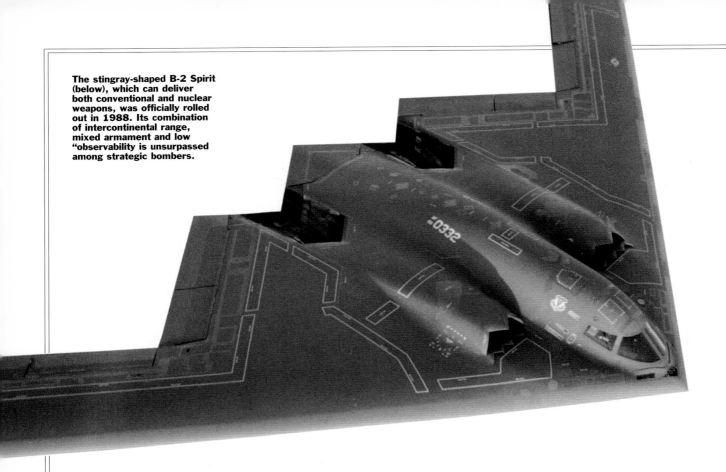

The stingray-shaped B-2 Spirit (below), which can deliver both conventional and nuclear weapons, was officially rolled out in 1988. Its combination of intercontinental range, mixed armament and low "observability is unsurpassed among strategic bombers.

B-2
Spirit

• **Northrop**

The triangular and exotic airborne-fighting machine known as the stealth bomber is perhaps the world's most versatile warplane.

In 1935, an exotic form of radio known as radar revolutionized aerial combat. In its most basic form, radar consists of a transmitter that sends a narrowly focused beam of high-frequency electromagnetic energy into space, a receiver that listens for energy that bounces off objects in the path of the beam, and a display that shows the object's location. Radar makes aircraft detectable at great distance, in the dark and through fog. During World War II, the British Chain Home radar system alerted the Royal Air Force to approaching German aircraft. Radar that scanned the ocean for periscopes helped to end the terror of Nazi U-boats, radar-aimed guns protected B-29s during

night missions, and radar navigation and targeting made bombing accurate in all weather conditions.

In the early 1970s, the Defense Advanced Research Projects Agency, a little-known branch of the Department of Defense, obtained intelligence that Soviet scientists believed it possible to build a plane that would be invisible to radar. After a series of experiments proved the theory workable, the Air Force committed to building two "stealth" aircraft, the Lockheed F-117 Nighthawk, a jet fighter discussed in chapter 3, and the Northrop B-2 Spirit bomber, which made its maiden flight on July 17, 1989.

At an average cost of $2 billion apiece, B-2s are

VITALS	
Designation	B-2A Spirit
Wingspan	172 ft.
Length	69 ft.
Gross Weight	336,500 pounds
Top Speed	High subsonic
Cruising Speed	High subsonic
Range	Approximately 7480 miles
Ceiling	Approximately 50,000 ft.

the most expensive aircraft ever built. Most of the cost of the plane is related to the exotic materials used in its construction. Resembling a giant bat, the B-2 uses sweeping curves to diffuse and deflect most of the electromagnetic energy that strikes it from radar transmitters. Layered carbon composite in the frame and ferrite-based honeycombs in the skin absorb still more of the incoming radar waves. Consequently, the signal returned by a B-2 is about the size of that of a large bird.

Radar is not the only system capable of detecting aircraft, however. Aircraft engines produce heat—electromagnetic energy in the infrared region below the detection frequencies of the human eye, and infrared sensors can readily detect hot engines, clear standouts against the comparatively cold sky. To hide this "infrared signature," a venting system combines hot exhaust from the B-2's four 118-GE-100 General Electric turbofans—which generate a total of 69,200 pounds of thrust—with the outside air and disperses the much cooler mixture behind the aircraft. And as a final, albeit low-tech, stealth technique, the B-2 operates at speeds below Mach 1 to avoid tipping off defenders with telltale sonic booms.

The high cost of flying and maintaining the B-2 limits its use to bombing only the most critical targets, such as enemy command and control posts. Because of the enormous damage to national security that might occur if a stealth

bomber were to fall into the wrong hands, B-2s operate only from within the United States—currently Whiteman Air Force Base in Missouri. The extreme range of the B-2 more than compensates for its protected location in the American heartland. In a historic U.S. Air Force flight by Maj. Chris Inman and Maj. Steve Moulton of the 509th Bomb Wing on July 6 and 7, 1997, a B-2 flew an astounding 15,000 miles during a 37-hour, 36-minute round-trip mission from Whiteman to a hypothetical target near Guam.

In an actual attack, the B-2 can release up to 40,000 pounds of conventional or nuclear ordnance—ranging from "dumb" bombs to cruise missiles with a range of hundreds of miles—from rotary launchers in two side-by-side weapons bays.

With the B-2 Spirit, the Air Force has finally achieved the goal that first lured the military to the sky: the ability to conceivably end a war before the enemy can land its first blow.

For all of its state-of-the-art technology, the B-2 (above) requires constant maintenance. After every flight, a technician carefully examines the 10,000-sq.-ft. surface of the aircraft for any damage to its radar-defying skin.

B-2A Spirit

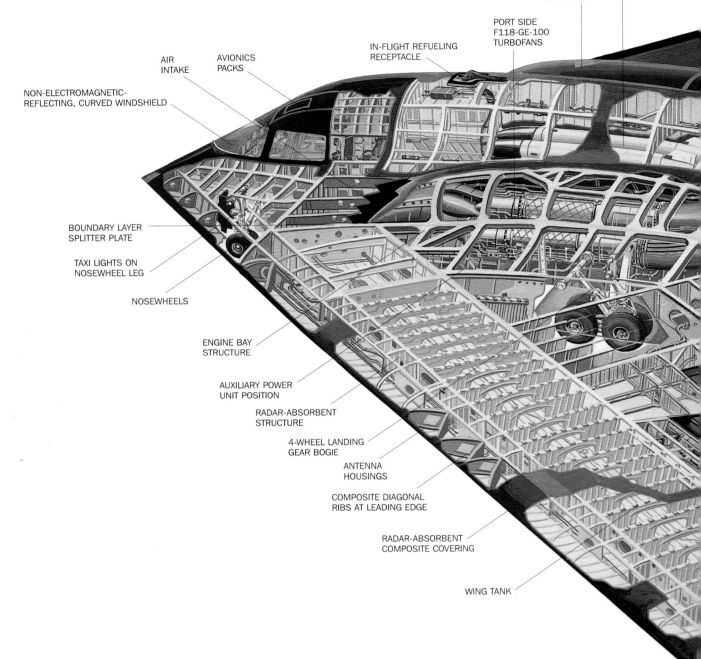

8 NUCLEAR WEAPONS ON STARBOARD ROTARY WEAPONS DISPENSER

SECONDARY AIR INTAKES

PORT SIDE F118-GE-100 TURBOFANS

IN-FLIGHT REFUELING RECEPTACLE

AIR INTAKE

AVIONICS PACKS

NON-ELECTROMAGNETIC-REFLECTING, CURVED WINDSHIELD

BOUNDARY LAYER SPLITTER PLATE

TAXI LIGHTS ON NOSEWHEEL LEG

NOSEWHEELS

ENGINE BAY STRUCTURE

AUXILIARY POWER UNIT POSITION

RADAR-ABSORBENT STRUCTURE

4-WHEEL LANDING GEAR BOGIE

ANTENNA HOUSINGS

COMPOSITE DIAGONAL RIBS AT LEADING EDGE

RADAR-ABSORBENT COMPOSITE COVERING

WING TANK

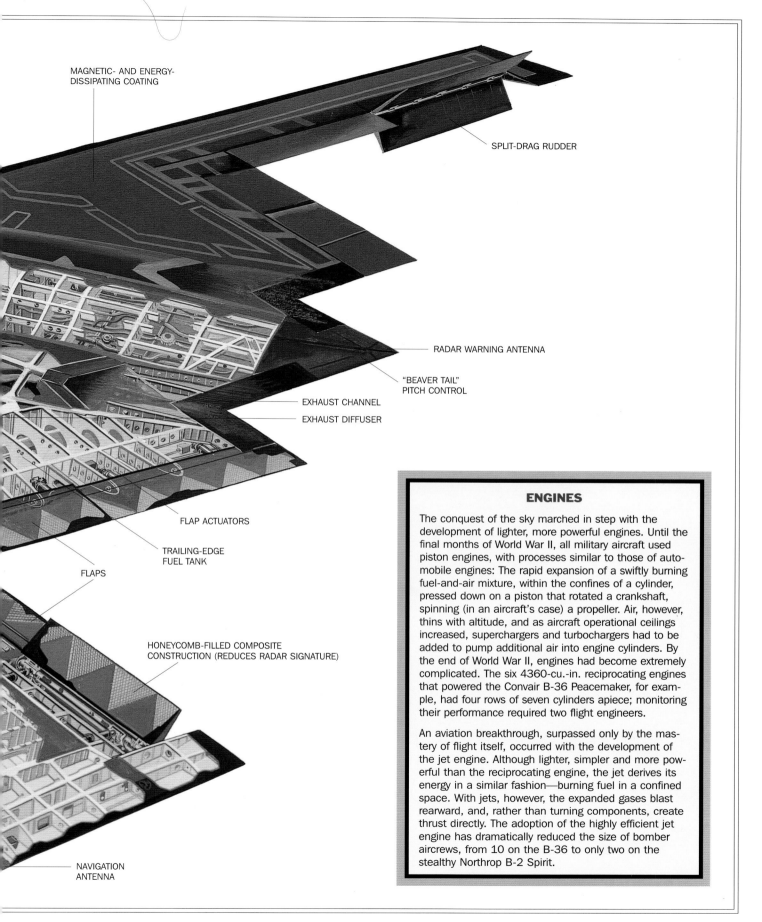

MAGNETIC- AND ENERGY-
DISSIPATING COATING

SPLIT-DRAG RUDDER

RADAR WARNING ANTENNA

"BEAVER TAIL"
PITCH CONTROL

EXHAUST CHANNEL

EXHAUST DIFFUSER

FLAP ACTUATORS

TRAILING-EDGE
FUEL TANK

FLAPS

HONEYCOMB-FILLED COMPOSITE
CONSTRUCTION (REDUCES RADAR SIGNATURE)

NAVIGATION
ANTENNA

ENGINES

The conquest of the sky marched in step with the development of lighter, more powerful engines. Until the final months of World War II, all military aircraft used piston engines, with processes similar to those of automobile engines: The rapid expansion of a swiftly burning fuel-and-air mixture, within the confines of a cylinder, pressed down on a piston that rotated a crankshaft, spinning (in an aircraft's case) a propeller. Air, however, thins with altitude, and as aircraft operational ceilings increased, superchargers and turbochargers had to be added to pump additional air into engine cylinders. By the end of World War II, engines had become extremely complicated. The six 4360-cu.-in. reciprocating engines that powered the Convair B-36 Peacemaker, for example, had four rows of seven cylinders apiece; monitoring their performance required two flight engineers.

An aviation breakthrough, surpassed only by the mastery of flight itself, occurred with the development of the jet engine. Although lighter, simpler and more powerful than the reciprocating engine, the jet derives its energy in a similar fashion—burning fuel in a confined space. With jets, however, the expanded gases blast rearward, and, rather than turning components, create thrust directly. The adoption of the highly efficient jet engine has dramatically reduced the size of bomber aircrews, from 10 on the B-36 to only two on the stealthy Northrop B-2 Spirit.

F-16s cruising over southern Europe

CHAPTER 3
Fighters

Four U.S. Army Air Corps P-12s (left) brought up the rear in a somewhat ragged formation of eight; between 1929 and 1932 Boeing produced 366 P-12s for the U.S. military. (The Navy also deployed the P-12, under the designation F4B.) In 1931, Boeing unveiled the P-26 (above), the United States' first all-metal monoplane "pursuit" plane, which pilots affectionately dubbed the "Peashooter."

Fighters

Velocity, maneuverability and firepower—the hallmarks of plane-versus-plane combat—define these lethal steeds, which rule the skies and confer the mantle of air superiority upon the men who fly them.

With the exception of digital computers, no complex machine, perhaps, has developed faster than the fighter. In half a century, planes designed to attack other planes have evolved from slow-moving boxes with a single gun to supersonic airframes with a deadly array of weapons.

Officially, the United States did not use the designation "fighter" until May 1948. Before the creation of the United States Air Force, the U.S. Army Air Forces and the U.S. Army Air Corps characterized airplanes that attacked airborne targets—balloons, blimps, planes and zeppelins—as "pursuit" aircraft. The first Americans to fly these planes acquired their aerial combat experience with British and French units that fought in Europe before the United States entered World

A British Sopwith Camel (above, foreground), the most successful Allied aircraft in World War I, chased down its German counterpart, the Fokker, over Europe during the Great War. The Sopwith Camel was credited with downing 1294 enemy planes in the war; the Fokker, created by Dutch designer Anthony Fokker (the "Flying Dutchman"), made legends out of Hermann Göring and Manfred von Richthofen.

War I. When America finally joined the fray, it possessed no combat-worthy aircraft, and the French-built SPAD XIII became the dominant U.S. aircraft for both air-to-air combat and missions that attacked troops on the ground. A quarter-century later, a new generation of pilots honed their skills in a similar scenario. Members of the American Volunteer Group, the Flying Tigers, were based in China and trained for missions against Japanese Zeroes months before the sneak attack at Pearl Harbor; the Tigers, however, flew an American plane, the then state-of-the-art Curtiss P-40 Warhawk. To avoid being caught unprepared again, several U.S. pursuit aircraft had been in the production pipeline years before World War II.

During and after World War II, five technical developments would stand out as milestones in the fighter's story: radar, the jet engine, the swept wing, computer control and stealth capability.

Radar gave pilots, and the anti-aircraft batteries that opposed them, the ability to "see" through the night and cloudy skies. In the Battle of Britain, radar pointed the Royal Air Force (RAF) in the direction of approaching German attackers, enabling it to organize its defenses to inflict maximum damage with comparatively meager resources. Radar-guided missiles would eventually make the machine gun and cannon obsolete, replacing the legendary close-quarter dogfight with stand-off combat fought from distances measured in tens of miles.

Jet engines delivered aircraft the gift of phenomenal speed and eventually made fighters simpler to maintain. At their heart, jets use relatively simple reaction engines that create an enormous amount of thrust relative to their size, weight and number of moving parts—and do so without a propeller. While all engines require air for combustion, the jet engine required none of the modifications needed by the reciprocating engines that dominated fighter design through the last months of World War II such as specially formulated high-octane gasoline and superchargers or turbochargers to maintain sufficient airflow into cylinders at high altitudes.

As powerful as early jet engines were, they alone could not propel an aircraft beyond the ultimate speed limit of the day, the sound barrier.

This benchmark, however, would soon be eclipsed, chiefly due to a discovery made by German scientists in the mid-1930s. Airplanes achieve flight because the slightly curved shape of their wings creates low-pressure areas as they move forward. At high speeds, these structures compress the air ahead of them, creating shock waves capable, it was soon learned, of actually destroying fast planes like the Lockheed P-38 Lightning. Wind-tunnel data from the Germans' experiments revealed that raking a straight wing backward would delay the build-up of this shock wave, permitting faster and, ultimately, supersonic flight.

Two Lockheed F-104 Starfighters (above) cruised in tandem en route to a USAF airshow in Florida. The Starfighter was the first production plane to reach Mach 2, twice the speed of sound, in level flight. It also held simultaneous records for speed, altitude and time-to-climb.

Among the most valued and versatile weapons in the Allies' World War II arsenal, P-47 Thunderbolts (above) functioned both as high-altitude escort fighters and low-level fighter-bombers. Boeing added a 20mm cannon to the F-4E Phantom II (right) after operational experience with its previous models in Vietnam; the popular Phantom served the Navy, the Air Force and the Marine Corps.

Research in aerodynamics led to further refinements of wing design, including the creation of wings so delicately poised between lift and stall positions that even the most skilled pilot couldn't keep the aircraft aloft. Then an emerging technology, the computer, brought control up to par with design and took over the moment-by-moment changes in the movements of a plane's control surfaces, which allowed high-tech aircraft to remain airborne. Thus, with the advent of the General Dynamics F-16 Fighting Falcon, the pilot did not so much fly the plane as point it in a particular direction.

The computer's superior plane-handling skills would also play a leading role in the virtual defeat of a fighter pilot's worst enemy: anti-aircraft radar. As early as the '30s, scientists had believed that disrupting the radar energy that impinges upon an airframe was theoretically possible. Now, the computer-controlled fly-by-wire systems developed for the F-16 keeps just such an airframe airborne, making the first radar-defeating fighter, the Lockheed F-117 Nighthawk, a stealthy reality. Additionally, computers have made possible a new generation of precision weapon systems that, among other technological marvels, can home in on their targets by recognizing their visual, infrared or radar signatures.

Technology has taken us to the twilight of this chapter in the fighter's history. The next Air Force fighter, the Lockheed Martin F-22 Raptor, may be the last flown by a human pilot. The structural integrity of the F-22 airframe and the power of its engines create G-forces at the very limits of human endurance. The ultimate 21st century flying machine may be just that—a machine.

Taking its name from the acronym of its French designers, le Société pour l'Aviation et ses Dérives, the SPAD XIII (above) was constructed in 1916 as an answer to the twin-gun German fighters of the day. It doubled the firepower of its predecessor, the SPAD VII, by sporting two machine guns with 400 rounds of ammunition each. France produced more than 2000 SPAD XIIIs before 1918.

SPAD XIII

• Société pour l'Aviation et ses Dérives

The SPAD XIII won the battle for the skies in World War I and forever established the military value of air power.

America's late entry into World War I, coupled with the virtual absence of a civil aviation industry, meant that the U.S. Army would have to buy its combat aircraft from its allies. For a bomber, the War Department turned to the British and adapted their de Havilland DH-4 for mass production with an American power plant, the 400-hp water-cooled Liberty engine. For the plane that we now call a fighter, Washington turned to the French, who, from the very beginning, had grasped the military value of air power and quickly applied the lessons learned in the opening months of the war to create faster, more agile and better-armed aircraft.

Early in the war, engineers had experimented with several types of engine design, but their radial air-cooled engines, in which the cylinders spun on a fixed driveshaft, and liquid-cooled engines, in which cylinders were placed in a line, were too large and heavy for the fast maneuvering characteristic of dogfights.

VITALS	
Designation	SPAD XIII
Wingspan	26 ft. 6 in.
Length	20 ft. 6 in.
Gross Weight	1888 pounds
Top Speed	135 mph
Cruising Speed	N/A
Range	250 miles
Ceiling	20,000 ft.

It was Marc Birkigt, cofounder and chief designer of the automotive company Hispano-Suiza, who hit upon the solution: a compact water-cooled engine with its cylinders arranged in a V configuration. Upon learning of Birkigt's new 150-hp creation, SPAD's Louis Béchereau started work on a new project of his own that would use the new engine—the SPAD VII. It entered service on the front in the fall of 1916, and its performance was so well received that the French immediately deployed 5500 of the new "fighting scouts."

Birkigt continued to wring more and more power from the Hispano-Suiza V-8. Béchereau took advantage of what was then a 200-hp engine to build an even faster, higher-flying, more agile and better-armed aircraft, the SPAD XIII, which made its first flight on April 4, 1917. By the end of the war, the most advanced Hispano-Suiza engine produced 220 hp. This gave the SPAD XIII a 135-mph top speed, a 20,000-ft. service ceiling and—coupled with the its rugged airframe—the capacity for faster climbs and steeper dives. Beefing up the fire-power to twin synchronized Vickers .303-cal. machine guns additionally helped the SPAD XII meet the challenge of German two-gun aircraft.

After witnessing their performance in combat,

(continued)

U.S. ace Eddie V. Rickenbacker (above) posed in his SPAD XIII during World War I. The U.S. Air Service began purchasing these pioneering dogfighters from the French in March 1918, and by year's end had acquired 893 of the twin-gun biplanes.

the Belgians, British, Italians and Russians adopted the plane, as did the American Expeditionary Force. By the end of the war, nine companies had built 8472 SPAD XIIIs, and another 10,000 were on order. About half of these were scheduled to be built in the United States.

By Armistice Day, SPAD-series aircraft had proved themselves the best of their contemporaries; historians would later judge that the SPAD XIII was a critical factor in tipping the balance of air superiority to the Allies. The plane had an even more powerful influence on the future of American combat aviation. In the years that followed World War I, the men who had flown SPAD XIIIs to victory in Europe also flew into the pages of aviation history and formed the backbone of the U.S. Army Air Corps. Seventy-one Americans had become aces, pilots credited with five or more enemy kills, led by Congressional Medal of Honor-winner Capt. Eddie Rickenbacker, with 26. Their success over the skies of France would help to elevate the role of air power within the military and ultimately aid in the creation of the world's most powerful air force.

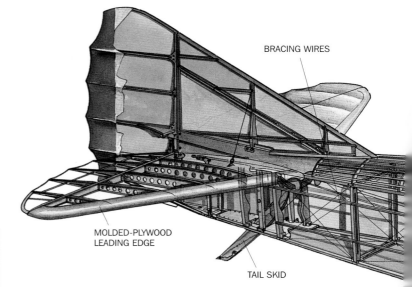

BRACING WIRES

MOLDED-PLYWOOD
LEADING EDGE

TAIL SKID

ENLISTED PILOTS

Unlike today, in the early days of aviation it was frequently possible for enlisted men to become pilots and earn their wings. America's top World War I ace, Capt. Eddie Rickenbacker, began his career as a mechanic before learning to fly a SPAD XIII fighter in France. When the Army demobilized after the war, flying became an officers' club—so much so that in 1926 and again in 1941, Congress passed legislation to force the Army to train more enlisted men as pilots. The Army essentially ignored the 1926 directive but at the start of World War II created the sergeant-pilot program for high school graduates. This initiative ended in 1942 when the Army dropped the college requirement for aviation cadets. The 2576 sergeant pilots who had already graduated were promoted to 2nd Lieutenants but not before 217 of them had flown combat missions as enlisted men.

According to the U.S. Air Force Museum, a total of 4150 enlisted men earned their wings; 18 went on to become aces. On October 14, 1947, one of the young men who had begun his flight training in the Army sergeant-pilot program conquered one of the last frontiers of aviation: As a captain in the U.S. Air Force, Charles "Chuck" Yeager became the first person to fly faster than the speed of sound.

Currently, the Air Force and Navy allow only officers to fly. The Army, however, permits men and women holding the rank of warrant officer to pilot helicopters.

SPAD XIII

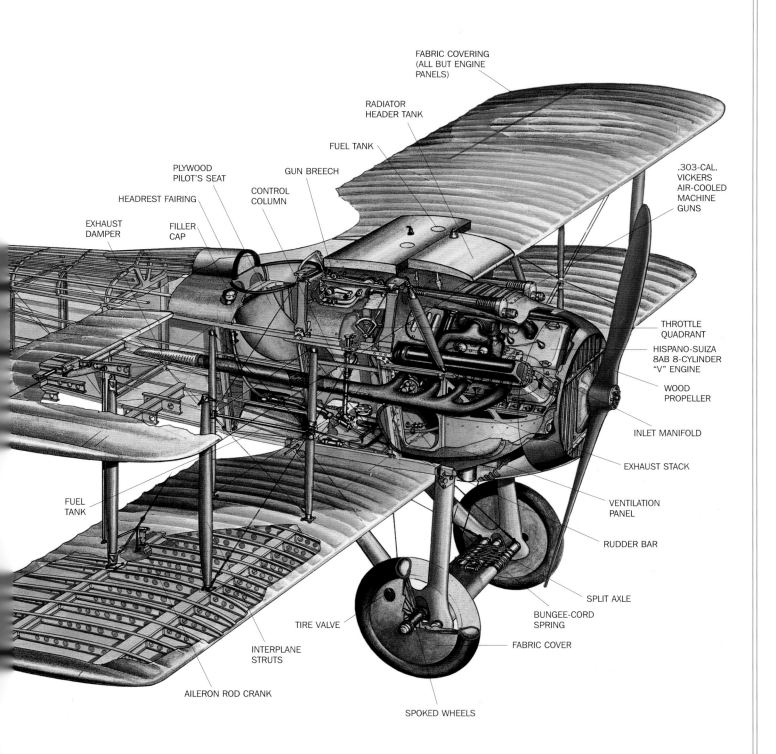

FABRIC COVERING
(ALL BUT ENGINE
PANELS)

RADIATOR
HEADER TANK

FUEL TANK

GUN BREECH

PLYWOOD
PILOT'S SEAT

CONTROL
COLUMN

HEADREST FAIRING

FILLER
CAP

EXHAUST
DAMPER

.303-CAL.
VICKERS
AIR-COOLED
MACHINE
GUNS

THROTTLE
QUADRANT

HISPANO-SUIZA
8AB 8-CYLINDER
"V" ENGINE

WOOD
PROPELLER

INLET MANIFOLD

EXHAUST STACK

VENTILATION
PANEL

RUDDER BAR

FUEL
TANK

SPLIT AXLE

BUNGEE-CORD
SPRING

TIRE VALVE

FABRIC COVER

INTERPLANE
STRUTS

AILERON ROD CRANK

SPOKED WHEELS

The twin-engine, twin-boom P-38 Lightning destroyed more enemy aircraft in air-to-air combat in the Pacific theater than any other Allied plane. The Lightning also achieved more 'firsts' than any other U.S. fighter: The P-38 was the first plane to fly against Germany in World War II, the first fighter to make a round-trip mission over Berlin, and the first to fly over Tokyo, among other milestones.

P-38
Lightning

• **Lockheed**

Developed in secrecy by Lockheed, the Lightning became the only U.S. pursuit plane in continuous production throughout World War II.

At the start of World War II, the Lockheed P-38 Lightning was the Army's largest, heaviest and deadliest fighter. A single wartime statistic summarizes its effectiveness: It was the plane flown by America's two top-scoring aces, Maj. Richard Bong, who scored 40 kills, and Maj. Tommy McGuire, with 38.

Developed in the late 1930s under secrecy, the P-38 represented a radical and daring departure from previous fighter design. Nearly twice the size of the fighters of the day, the P-38's signature was its distinctive twin-boom airframe. Its pilot and, on later models, a radar operator, were nestled in a cockpit that merged into the rear of the wing. Equally radical, but only visible on takeoffs and landings, was the retractable tricycle landing gear

VITALS	
Designation	P-38J Lightning
Wingspan	52 ft.
Length	37 ft. 10 in.
Gross Weight	17,500 pounds
Top Speed	414 mph
Cruising Speed	275 mph
Range	1100 miles
Ceiling	40,000 ft.

that has since become standard on all commercial and military aircraft.

German pilots aptly nicknamed the P-38—the Army's most heavily armed fighter—the "fork-tailed devil." Ahead of the pilot, in space normally occupied by the engine, it held a veritable arsenal. Production models, powered by two 1475-hp Allison V-1710 engines, fired at enemy aircraft with a 20mm cannon and four .50-cal. machine guns. As the Lightning swooped from 25,000 ft. at 414 mph, a one-second burst of coordinated fire created a lethal wall of metal that shredded any aircraft in its sights. Beneath its wings it could carry either bombs or rockets. Lockheed also took pioneering steps in pilot protection with the P-38, including cockpit armor and self-sealing fuel tanks.

Beyond its physical attributes, the creation of the P-38 represented a change in the way the aviation industry and the War Department conducted business, marking the ascendancy of the defense industry over the military in defining future generations of aircraft. Previously, American industry built what the government ordered, and then only after Uncle Sam had signed the check. When Pearl Harbor drew America into World War II, the U.S.

Army Air Corps was flush with short-range Curtiss P-40s because its plans did not perceive an attack by Japan as a viable threat. Indeed, at the time the P-38 was being planned, America was happily shipping Japan perhaps the most critical material it would need to wage war on the United States: scrap steel.

A small number of Air Corps officers and executives at Lockheed Aircraft, however, saw the world as a more hostile place: While the Army was purchasing P-40s for about $45,000 each, Lockheed was investing an astounding $6 million to develop the P-38. The first prototype, the XP-38, made its maiden flight on January 27, 1939, and had its public debut little more than two weeks later when the Army and Lockheed staged what they hoped would be a record-breaking cross-country

(continued)

The two-seat P-38M (above), painted black and rigged with a bulbous nose-mounted radome, provided the USAAF with a speedy, high-performance night fighter.

flight. It ended badly, however, with the pilot hitting a tree and crash-landing into a golf course sand trap adjacent to Mitchell Field in New York. Luckily, he survived. That debacle notwithstanding, the Army placed an order for 13 test aircraft, designated YP-38s. With the United States formally at peace (despite the outbreak of war in Europe), the Army had the luxury of time to refine the P-38's design by experimenting with different weapons configurations. The first production models—35 P-38Ds and 210 P-38Es—arrived two months before the sneak attack on Pearl Harbor but were absent from the line of fire on that fateful December morning.

Designed as fighter-bombers, the P-38 could carry sufficient bombs and rockets beneath its wings to sink a small ship. Equipping the plane with a pair of wing-mounted drop tanks increased its fuel capacity from 410 to 1010 gal. and extended its range to 1100 miles for long-range bomber escort duty. As the war and technology progressed, the P-38 evolved into new models, including the two-seat P-38M radar-guided night fighter, a harbinger of the postwar fighters to come.

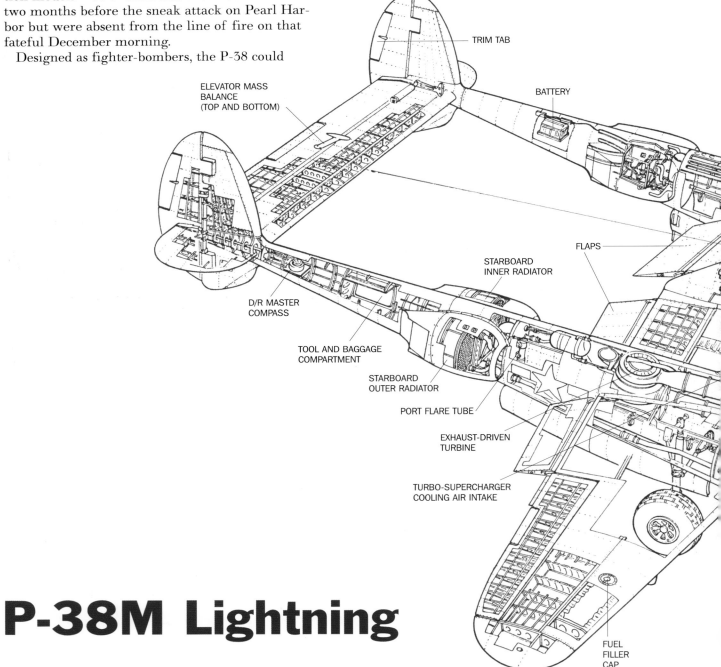

TRIM TAB

BATTERY

ELEVATOR MASS
BALANCE
(TOP AND BOTTOM)

FLAPS

STARBOARD
INNER RADIATOR

D/R MASTER
COMPASS

TOOL AND BAGGAGE
COMPARTMENT

STARBOARD
OUTER RADIATOR

PORT FLARE TUBE

EXHAUST-DRIVEN
TURBINE

TURBO-SUPERCHARGER
COOLING AIR INTAKE

FUEL
FILLER
CAP

P-38M Lightning

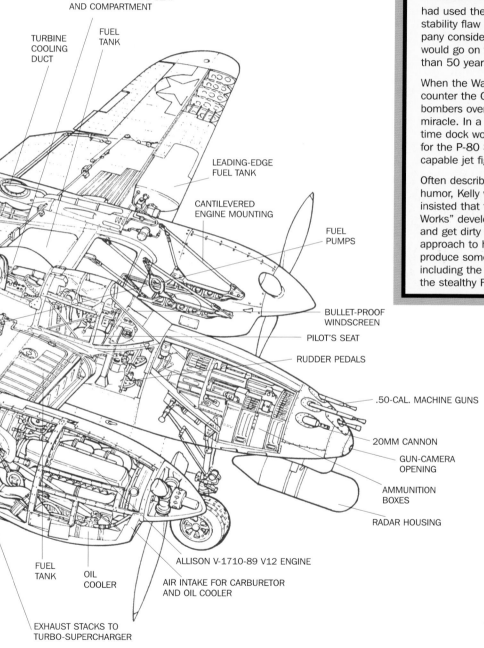

RADAR OPERATOR'S SEAT
AND COMPARTMENT

TURBINE
COOLING
DUCT

FUEL
TANK

LEADING-EDGE
FUEL TANK

CANTILEVERED
ENGINE MOUNTING

FUEL
PUMPS

BULLET-PROOF
WINDSCREEN

PILOT'S SEAT

RUDDER PEDALS

.50-CAL. MACHINE GUNS

20MM CANNON

GUN-CAMERA
OPENING

AMMUNITION
BOXES

RADAR HOUSING

FUEL
TANK

OIL
COOLER

AIR INTAKE FOR CARBURETOR
AND OIL COOLER

ALLISON V-1710-89 V12 ENGINE

EXHAUST STACKS TO
TURBO-SUPERCHARGER

KELLY JOHNSON (1910-1990)

By the time Clarence "Kelly" Johnson was 33, he had already established his reputation as the Leonardo da Vinci of aviation—his Lockheed P-38 Lightning was the most maneuverable plane in the sky. As a 23-year old engineering student at the University of Michigan, Kelly had used the same twin-tail design to correct a critical stability flaw in the Lockheed Electra, saving the company considerable financial trouble in the process. He would go on to be affiliated with Lockheed for more than 50 years.

When the War Department needed a fast plane to counter the German jet aircraft that threatened Allied bombers over Europe, they turned to Kelly to deliver a miracle. In a remarkable 143 days, the scrappy one-time dock worker produced Lulu Belle, the prototype for the P-80 Shooting Star, America's first combat-capable jet fighter.

Often described as W. C. Fields without a sense of humor, Kelly willingly shared his magic formula. He insisted that the engineers who worked in his "Skunk Works" development center leave their drawing boards and get dirty on the shop floor. This unusual hands-on approach to high-performance aircraft design would produce some of the world's most advanced airplanes, including the high-flying U-2 and SR-71 spyplanes and the stealthy F-117 Nighthawk.

P-40
Warhawk

• Curtiss

Technologically inferior to its European peers, the scrappy Warhawk paved the way for the ultimate U.S. prop fighter, the P-51 Mustang.

The Curtiss P-40 Warhawk, which made its first flight on April 4, 1940, was America's first mass-produced single-seat fighter. The "P" indicated that the U.S. Army Air Corps categorized the plane as a pursuit aircraft, a designation given to fighters throughout the war. The prefix "F" for fighter would not appear until 1948. Regardless of identification schemes, P-40s were the first U.S. Army Air Forces planes to fight in World War II. In the midst of the chaos of Japan's attack on Pearl Harbor, four P-40s managed to stage a limited counterattack. Across the International Date Line, these aircraft also stood against the Land of the

Rising Sun at Luzon when the Japanese attacked the Philippine Islands.

The P-40s were the first and staunchest defenders of America on virtually every battlefront. In addition to their small but symbolically important role during Pearl Harbor, P-40s fought in the Aleutian Islands, Italy, Africa, the Middle East and the Far East. During the plane's production history, some 14,000 P-40s would fly in the air forces of 28 countries, including Russia and Britain. And, as we will see later in this chapter, British attempts to buy more P-40s would lead to the development of the greatest propeller-driven fighter of all time,

A pilot peered out of the "greenhouse" cockpit of his P-40D Warhawk, America's primary fighter at the start of World War II. Warhawks fought the Japanese at Pearl Harbor and powered the 99th Fighter Squadron, the Army Air Force's first all-black unit, in 1943.

the North American P-51 Mustang.

The P-40 traces its airframes to the 1920s-era Curtiss Hawk. In 1939, Britain and France flew Curtiss Hawk Model 75s against Germany. These planes quickly proved themselves inferior to the faster, more heavily armed German Messerschmitt 109s, however. This revelation was quite a wake-up call for the American Air Corps: Its year-old fleet of 243 P-36s—Hawk Model-75 derivatives—was already obsolete. Although two P-36s also flew against Japanese attackers at Pearl Harbor on the morning of December 7, 1941, surviving P-36s were reassigned to non-combatant training and courier duties. Early retirement of the P-36 put the more advanced Curtiss P-40 at the tip of the spear when the United States declared war against Germany and Japan.

The famous World War II "Flying Tiger" unit painted the noses of their P-40 Warhawks (above) to resemble the snarling snouts of sharks. A volunteer outfit, the Tigers defended the Burma Road in southern China against the Japanese before U.S. forces officially joined the war.

The P-40 represented a significant improvement over the P-36 but still fell short of the performance of Germany's Me 109 and Japan's Mitsubishi A6M Zero-Sen fighters. The source of its improvement as well as its limitation, lay in its 12-cylinder inline Allison V-1710 water-cooled engine. Derived from a 1930s-era engine that powered airships, the V-1710 was the product of an Army research-and-development program aimed at producing a higher-power liquid-cooled engine. The first V-1710s, rated at 1000 hp, had been used in experimental aircraft in 1932. During World War II, the engine's output was steadily increased to as high as 1475 hp. The engine was not only the primary power plant for the P-40 and the Lockheed P-38 Lightning, but also the earliest versions of the P-51 Mustang. Superior though they were, the Allison engines had a critical shortcoming—they were only rated to fly to 12,000 ft., making the planes they powered proverbial sitting ducks for attacks from above.

A solution would come with the engine that gave the P-40 its nickname. In 1941, P-40s were equipped with British-built Rolls-Royce Merlin 28 engines outfitted with a single-stage, two-speed supercharger. Despite decreasing oxygen levels at higher altitudes, these new engines could produce 1120 hp at 18,500 ft., and later models extended the P-40's service ceiling to a lofty 30,000 ft. While these aircraft were hardly converted into super-fighters, the "Warhawks" soaring at these higher altitudes were, at the very least, contenders in the skies.

With their six .50-cal. machine guns blazing, P-40s were the cornerstone of U.S. air power during America's first year of World War II. Although virtually every plane a P-40 encountered in combat could fly faster, climb more swiftly or out-maneuver it in a dogfight, the Warhawk possessed the single most important characteristic needed to win a battle: When the war broke out, they were ready to fight.

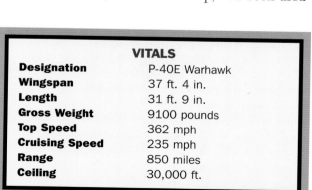

VITALS	
Designation	P-40E Warhawk
Wingspan	37 ft. 4 in.
Length	31 ft. 9 in.
Gross Weight	9100 pounds
Top Speed	362 mph
Cruising Speed	235 mph
Range	850 miles
Ceiling	30,000 ft.

A formation of F-47Ns (above)—the P designation was changed to F in 1948—cruised through the clouds over northern Georgia. This long-range escort was the last kind of Thunderbolt created; more than 1800 were built. The P-47 was one of the most famous fighters of the Second World War. From 1943-45, P-47s dropped more than 130,000 tons of bombs and fired 135 million belts of ammo.

P-47
Thunderbolt

• Republic

With the ability to withstand punishing combat damage and stay aloft, the heavy-duty P-47 excelled in almost every theater of WWII.

For those who saw the hulking beast squatting on the runway, it was hard to imagine that the Republic P-47 Thunderbolt could fly at all, let alone fly better than most other World War II-era fighters. Aircrews called it the "Jug," a shortened reference to its juggernaut-like dimensions; pilots called it the "Unbreakable." Protected by all-around armor, P-47 fliers returned with hair-raising tales of death-defying encounters. The sheer strength of the Thunderbolt brought the plane home despite structural damage that would have shredded less physically capable aircraft. All of this protection came at a price in terms of weight, however. Fueled and armed, some P-47 models

weighed nearly 10 tons, more than twice as much as most fighters of the time. The only planes with more heft that lifted off from World War II runways were multiengine aircraft.

The P-47 was large as well as heavy. British pilots recall recoiling at the sight of the tip of the Thunderbolt's wing, which landed about level with the cockpits of their Spitfires. Despite (and in many ways because of) its ungainly dimensions, the P-47 could fly faster and dive faster than anything the Luftwaffe could put in the sky—a considerable advantage.

The idea for the P-47 emerged in the summer of 1940, when it was becoming clear that

VITALS	
Designation	P-47D Thunderbolt
Wingspan	40 ft. 9 in.
Length	36 ft. 2 in.
Max. Weight	19,400 pounds
Top Speed	433 mph
Cruising Speed	350 mph
Range	1030 miles
Ceiling	42,000 ft.

German dominance in the skies over Europe would require the Allies to build larger, faster aircraft to escort strategic bombers and achieve air superiority. By the early 1940s, fighter design had coalesced around two liquid-cooled inline engines, the Allison V-1710 and the Rolls-Royce Merlin. Though powerful, these were not the largest engines available. Pratt & Whitney had been working in earnest on a 2000-hp, air-cooled radial engine with 12 cylinders aligned in two-rows. Alexander Kartveli, the chief engineer for Republic Aviation, believed the Double Wasp offered precisely the performance the Army needed for its next fighter. On May 6, 1941, 11 months after Kartveli put his first ideas on paper, the prototype XP-47B was ready to fly. It performed better than its bulky dimensions suggested and faster than even Kartveli calculated— a remarkable 412 mph.

Gearing up for production took longer than anticipated—the prototypes suffered an unusual amount of "teething" trouble, including a tendency of some of its control surfaces to freeze at high altitudes—and the first P-47s did not arrive in England until early 1943. The initial results were disastrous.

Success in aerial combat depends not only on the pilot's skill but also on the speed and agility of his aircraft. The Thunderbolt was certainly fast but hardly nimble, with an unfortunate tendency to spin during tight turns at low altitudes. New tactics evolved to take advantage of the P-47's diving abilities, however. Pilots were trained to pounce down on their targets with their eight wing-mounted .50-cal. Browning machine guns blazing. If they missed their targets, they simply tried to regain altitude and dive again. It was a crude but effective tactic—between the spring of 1943 and the end of World War II in August 1945, P-47 Thunderbolts were credited with destroying nearly 12,000 enemy aircraft.

The tactics that made the Thunderbolt an effective plane-to-plane fighter worked even better against ground targets. In bombing runs, P-47s hit more than 6000 tanks and other armored vehicles. They also engaged in strategic bombing against German railroads, claiming kills against some 9000 locomotives. Perhaps the most remarkable P-47 statistic of all is their survival rate. Living up to their reputation of being virtually indestructible, less than one percent of the Thunderbolts sent on combat missions were lost to enemy fire.

A serviceman from the 19th Fighter Squadron/318th Fighter Group (above) smiled in front of the "nose art" on his P-47 on le Shima island in 1945. Scantily clad women were often the subject of paintings that adorned Allied aircraft in the Second World War.

A squadron of P-51 Mustangs from the 352nd Fighter Group (above) occupied a Fourth Fighter Group airfield in Europe on June 20, 1944, before taking off on a mission over Russia. The P-51 distinguished itself in the Pacific theater as well as in Europe, providing the range, speed and durability necessary to escort heavy bombers on long-range missions.

P-51
Mustang

• North American

If one plane can be said to have tipped the balance of the air war in Europe during World War II, it is the Allies' P-51 Mustang.

Aviation enthusiasts speak fondly of the North American P-51 Mustang as the perfect marriage of airframe, engine and armaments. It is a curious epitaph for a plane with such an unorthodox genesis. As with many war stories, the saga of the P-51 began in 1939, the year World War II erupted in Europe. Hitler's rapid success jolted defense planners to the realization that Britain needed more fighter aircraft faster than the country's belea-

guered industrial capacity would permit. To fill the shortfall, the British Air Purchasing Commission decided to purchase export versions of the Curtiss P-40, which were then built by North American Aviation.

North American Aviation made an interesting counter-offer: It proposed that its engineering group, which included former Messerschmitt designer Edgar Schmued, create an entirely new

VITALS	
Designation	P-51D Mustang
Wingspan	37 ft.
Length	32 ft. 3 in.
Max. Weight	12,100 pounds
Top Speed	437 mph
Cruising Speed	275 mph
Range	1000 miles
Ceiling	41,900 ft.

fighter for the RAF. The British agreed with one condition: The aircraft would have to be completed in 120 days. Technically, North American delivered the plane in 117 days. An airframe, alas, cannot fly by itself; it needs an engine, and the Allison V-1710 powerplant had yet to be delivered. After a six-week delay, the engine finally arrived, and on May 4, 1940, the experimental XP-51 took off to begin the last chapter in the history of the propeller-driven fighter.

Pilots in the U.K. were pleased with the results—the P-51 could outperform the British Spitfire—and the RAF ordered 150 of the new planes. Not completely satisfied, however, they fit several with the 12-cylinder Rolls-Royce Merlin engine, which afforded the P-51 a higher service ceiling. Impressed with the improvement, the U.S. Army began ordering Merlin-equipped P-51s and, before the end of the war, purchased nearly 15,000 Mustangs in various configurations. The most advanced model, the P-51H, could fly at a zippy 487 mph and cruise at 25,000 ft.

Mustangs were configured with almost every imaginable weapons package, as dive bombers, ground attack and aerial reconnaissance planes, trainers and transports. However, for the U.S. Army their most important role was as a long-range fighter.

There is an old saying to the effect that in matters of war, amateurs talk strategy, aficionados

(continued)

Two airmen from the First Air Commando Group (above) piloted their P-51 Mustangs over the rugged mountains of Burma during World War II. Among long-range, propeller-driven escort fighters, the Mustangs, with their powerful British-made engines, had no peer.

P-51D Mustang

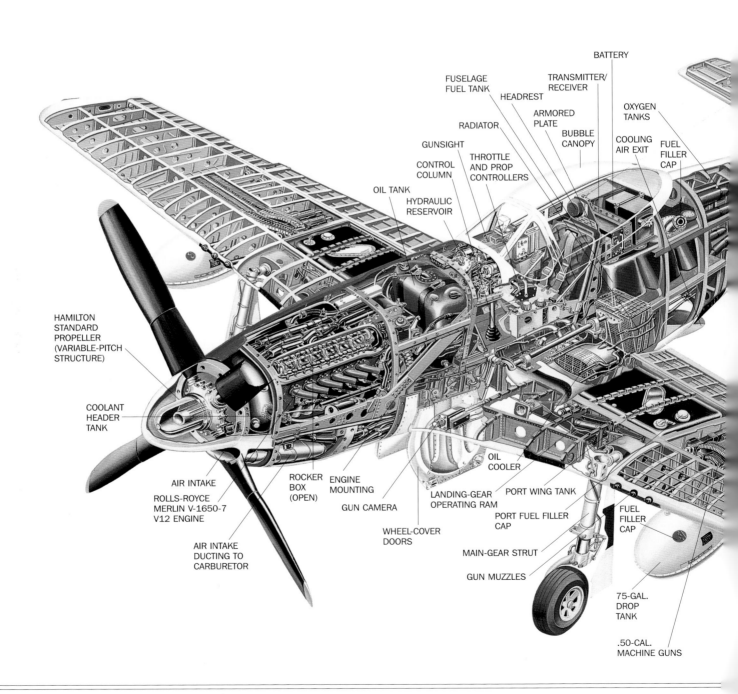

BATTERY

FUSELAGE
FUEL TANK

TRANSMITTER/
RECEIVER

HEADREST

OXYGEN
TANKS

RADIATOR

ARMORED
PLATE

BUBBLE
CANOPY

COOLING
AIR EXIT

FUEL
FILLER
CAP

GUNSIGHT

THROTTLE
AND PROP
CONTROLLERS

CONTROL
COLUMN

OIL TANK

HYDRAULIC
RESERVOIR

HAMILTON
STANDARD
PROPELLER
(VARIABLE-PITCH
STRUCTURE)

COOLANT
HEADER
TANK

AIR INTAKE

ROLLS-ROYCE
MERLIN V-1650-7
V12 ENGINE

ROCKER
BOX
(OPEN)

ENGINE
MOUNTING

GUN CAMERA

OIL
COOLER

PORT WING TANK

LANDING-GEAR
OPERATING RAM

PORT FUEL FILLER
CAP

FUEL
FILLER
CAP

AIR INTAKE
DUCTING TO
CARBURETOR

WHEEL-COVER
DOORS

MAIN-GEAR STRUT

GUN MUZZLES

75-GAL.
DROP
TANK

.50-CAL.
MACHINE GUNS

talk tactics and professionals talk logistics. Nowhere was this more true than in the conduct of the air war in Europe by the U.S. Army's 8th Air Force. Its Boeing B-17 Flying Fortresses and Consolidated B-24 Liberators flew under the protection of British Spitfires, Lockheed P-38 Lightnings and Republic P-47 Thunderbolts. The ranges of the bombers and fighters were seriously mismatched;

the bombers were forced to complete the last leg of their missions alone, exposed to German fighters with only their own defensive armaments to counter the threat. In December 1943 the arrival of P-51 Mustangs suddenly changed the equation. The P-51D, the most widely used model, powered by 1695-hp Packard-built Merlin V-1650-7 engines, packed six wing-mounted machine guns and more than 1800 rounds of .50-cal. ammunition; its 1000-mile range provided formidable fighter cover nearly as far as the Russian border for U.K.-based bombers. Herman Göring, chief of the Luftwaffe, is said to have once remarked: "When I saw Mustangs over Berlin, I knew that the air war was lost."

More than a half-century after sweeping the skies of Europe, the North American P-51 Mustang remains the epitome of the propeller-driven fighter. Mustangs represented one of those rare instances in which several technologies reach their individual peaks and merge in near-perfect harmony. Even after the arrival of jet aircraft, the U.S. Air Force would continue to fly the Mustang, redesignated the F-51. An impressive number of the more than 14,000 Mustangs acquired by the Army remain, lovingly cared for by enthusiasts, including some of the pilots who originally flew them over the war-clouded skies of Europe.

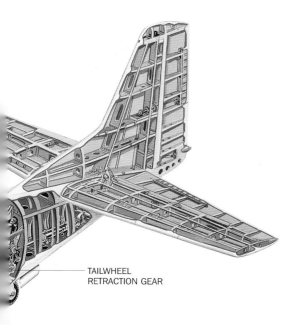

TAILWHEEL
RETRACTION GEAR

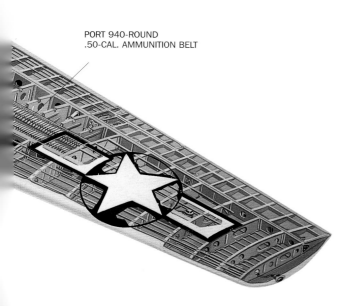

PORT 940-ROUND
.50-CAL. AMMUNITION BELT

IN PM'S WORDS
Secrets of Super-Speed

"Ordinary air, so familiar to us that we hardly ever think about it, is a temperamental mysterious substance to the men who design our high speed aircraft … .

"An outstanding example of how aerodynamicists and engineers are building speed into the design of a plane is North American Aviation's P-51 Mustang fighter. This plane has an announced ceiling of 40,000 feet and a top speed of around 425 mph. It is a large, heavy airplane and yet it offers no more resistance to the air than would a flat plate three and a half square feet in area. To the air, the P-51 is smaller than nine pages of this magazine laid side by side.

"To achieve this startling effect the North American Aviation aerodynamic staff did more than simply design a clean and streamlined plane. In half a dozen different ways they tricked the atmosphere into helping boost the plane along instead of retarding its flight.

"They designed the air intake duct that leads to the carburetor in such a way that the air rams itself in. This supercharging effect is so pronounced that at 30,000 feet the engine breathes air that is equal in density to the atmosphere a full mile below."

—POPULAR MECHANICS, October 1944

The famous photo below, of a P-80B, provided a first-flight glimpse of the U.S. Army Air Forces' hot rod of a new fighter. The addition of sleek auxiliary fuel tanks under the wing tips actually reduced drag, rather than increased it.

P-80
Shooting Star

• **Lockheed**

America's first mass-produced jet entered the record books in November 1950 when it won the first jet-versus-jet combat encounter.

The Lockheed F-80 Shooting Star took military aviation from the propeller era into the jet age. It scraped against the edge of the sound barrier and later distinguished itself in combat as the victor of the first jet-to-jet dogfight, during the Korean War. In the uncertain peace that followed Korea, the F-80 found a second life as the T-33, the military's primary jet trainer.

The story of the Shooting Star began two months before Pearl Harbor, when Henry "Hap" Arnold, commanding general of the U.S. Army Air Forces, authorized construction of the country's first jet aircraft, the Bell P-59 Airacomet. Powered by a pair of General Electric engines based on a British design, the plane made its first flight in October 1942. In the spring of 1943, P-59s became the nucleus

around which the War Department formed the United States Army Air Forces 412th Fighter Group. Like the British and the Germans before them, the Americans had achieved jet-fighter capability. In truth, the P-59 was a bitter disappointment. Only 66 were built and none flew in combat.

The Army abandoned the P-59 and opted to contract with Lockheed Aircraft to build an entirely new jet fighter, powered by a 3000-pound-thrust de Havilland version of the Whittle turbojet engine. In a remarkable 143 days, Clarence "Kelly" Johnson, America's most influential aircraft designer, led a team that created the Shooting Star at Lockheed Aircraft's secret Skunk Works plant in Southern California; the P-80 made its first flight on January 8, 1944.

VITALS

Designation	F-80C Shooting Star
Wingspan	38 ft. 10½ in.
Length	34 ft. 6 in.
Max. Weight	16,856 pounds
Top Speed	580 mph
Cruising Speed	437 mph
Range	1090 miles
Ceiling	46,800 ft.

The Shooting Star outperformed anything with a propeller but exacted a terrible price. The 4000-pound-thrust General Electric engines that replaced the British engines frequently exploded on takeoff. This kind of accident, sadly, killed Congressional Medal of Honor-winner Maj. Richard I. Bong, who, with 40 victories to his credit, remains America's highest-scoring ace. In less than 3 years, more than 60 P-80s would be lost in development and training accidents, giving the new fighter a less than savory reputation.

The Army, to counter the threat posed by German Me 262 jet fighters, dispatched Shooting Stars despite their problems. Two P-80s based in Italy became operational in the weeks before the European war ended but never encountered the enemy. The 30 shipped to the Philippines had a more curious story. They arrived without the wing-tip fuel tanks needed to extend the planes' 780-mile range to within striking distance of Japan. By the time the tanks arrived, the island nation had surrendered.

In the brief respite before the Korean War broke out, a modified P-80 broke the world's speed record, flying at a then scorching 623.8 mph.

The Korean War marked the end of the P-80, by then designated the F-80, as a combat aircraft. In the opening days of the war, it was simply too fast to engage the more agile Russian-built Yak and Lavochkin in aerial combat. Several F-80 squadrons actually reverted to flying North American Mustangs, by then designated F-51s. A change to tactics that avoided close-in maneuvers, as well as six .50-cal. machine guns and eight 5-in. rockets, gave the F-80 control of the sky, but their dominance would be short-lived. Although a confrontation on November 10, 1950, above the Yalu River between an F-80C and a MiG-15—Russia's newest jet—yielded the first jet-versus-jet victory for American forces, it also revealed that the era of the Shooting Star's technological superiority had passed: The swept-wing MiGs were more maneuverable and 100 mph faster.

As more advanced American fighter jets entered the war, the single-seat F-80 was retired. An elongated version with a second seat would become the Lockheed F-94 Starfire, the first all-weather interceptor. Another two-seat version, the T-33, would become a popular jet trainer. Nearly 5900 T-33s would become the classroom for fighter pilots throughout the world.

This lucky F-80 (above) made it home after sustaining damage from its own launched rocket in the skies over Korea. The ground-breaking Shooting Star had more mundane missions, too: On June 22, 1946, two P-80s became the first turbojet-powered aircraft to deliver U.S. airmail.

Three North American F-86As (above), from Nellis Air Force Base in Nevada, scooted across partly cloudy skies in a tight formation. A Sabre of this type set a world speed record of 670.981 mph on September 1, 1948. In the Korean War, Sabre pilots achieved an impressive jet-to-jet victory record of 10 to 1 over their adversaries in Soviet-built MiGs.

P-86
Sabre

• North American

Handily meeting the swept-wing challenge of the MiG-15, the F-86 Sabre wrested air superiority from the North Koreans in short order.

From the very beginning, the United States Army and Navy battled over control of the skies, not only with enemies, but also with each other. Until World War II the Navy had successfully argued that its need to land planes at sea, equipped with folding wings and other modification for carrier operations, demanded entirely separate development programs. The surprising appearance of jet engines on the German Me 262 during the Second World War, however, introduced a limited degree of cooperation between the two services. The first Navy jets were Bell P-59 Airacomets, aircraft originally built for the Army, and as World War II ended, the Army turned to naval design for what

would become its first supersonic fighter, the North American F-86 Sabre.

During that time, the Army was puzzled by two entirely different aviation problems. The first mystery involved the surprisingly poor performance of America's first jet-powered aircraft, the P-59 Airacomet, which flew no faster than the best propeller-driven fighters. About the same time, designers of the Lockheed P-38 Lightning were troubled by reports that their distinctive-looking twin-boom aircraft were spontaneously disintegrating while in flight. Both problems were caused by an aerodynamic phenomenon that aircraft encounter at high speeds: As a plane approaches

Pilots from the U.S. Air Force 44th Fighter-Bomber Squadron (above) scrambled to their F-86 Sabres during an alert call in the Philippines in 1954. The Sabre was one of the most prolific fighters ever built: From 1947 to 1957, more than 9800 were produced worldwide.

the speed of sound, it compresses a considerable amount of air ahead of its wing. At the time, this additional resistance was limiting speed and increasing vibrations, which, under certain conditions, could cause an airframe to literally shake apart. The solution to both problems arrived immediately after the conclusion of the war in Europe. Recovered German engineering documents revealed that sweeping the wing of an aircraft backward from its perpendicular position would delay the onset of the "compressibility" effects to a higher speed.

Swept-wing aircraft could fly faster, but the new wing design also reduced the plane's low-speed stability. In wind-tunnel tests, North American devised a workable compromise: The wing of the P-86 was swept back at a 35-degree angle, and auto-deploying slats were added to its leading edge to provide additional stability at low speeds.

A swept-wing P-86, powered by a 3750-pound-thrust Allison engine, made its first flight on October 1, 1947. Six months later, in April 1948, an XP-86 prototype became the first turbojet aircraft to break the sound barrier when it briefly achieved supersonic speed during a dive. The newly created U.S. Air Force was impressed with the promise of the Sabre's performance and

ordered 221 of the planes, equipped with larger, 4850-pound-thrust General Electric engines. The first of these more powerful planes flew in May 1948. One month later, the Air Force renamed its pursuit aircraft "fighters," and the improved Sabre entered service as the F-86A.

Air Force units equipped with the Sabres—armed with six .50-cal. nose-mounted machine guns— began arriving in Korea in December 1950. Clearly superior to the MiG-15s, the Sabres destroyed nearly 800 of the Russian fighters at the cost of fewer than 80 Air Force planes. All 39 of the war's U.S. aces flew Sabres.

North American continued to modify the Sabre, adding a more powerful engine, better navigation systems and, with the F-86D, replacing its guns with two dozen 2.75-in. Mighty Mouse folding-fin rockets carried in a retractable tray in the fuselage. Throughout the 1950s, Sabres set a series of speed records and won several National Aircraft Show Bendix Trophies. In July 1953 one of the D-series planes became the first aircraft to fly at speeds over 700 mph. U.S. production ended in December 1956. Canada, Italy and Japan also built Sabres under license. The famous fighter would eventually be included in the air forces of some 20 nations.

VITALS	
Designation	F-86D Sabre
Wingspan	37 ft. 1 in.
Length	40 ft. 4 in.
Gross Weight	19,975 pounds
Top Speed	717 mph
Cruising Speed	550 mph
Range	800 miles
Ceiling	50,000 ft.

Heavily laden with blaze-orange ordnance and resembling a high-tech insect, the F-4B, above, was intimidating just sitting on the runway. The U.S. Navy loaned 29 of these planes, then designated F4H-1s, to the U.S. Air Force in 1962. After seeing the Navy plane's superiority over the USAF's chief fighter at the time, the Convair F-106A, Air Force officials placed an order for their own version.

F-4
Phantom II

• **McDonnell**

Adept at missions of air superiority, interdiction and close-air support, the F-4 became a prized possession of air forces everywhere.

In the early 1950s the McDonnell Aircraft Company undertook an exercise normally performed by admirals and generals. Its executives attempted to look into the future and envision possible air-combat scenarios involving the United States. Based on those projections, the company began engineering studies that would lead to the most versatile, and arguably the most important, fighter of the Cold War era, the McDonnell F-4 Phantom II.

Over its service life of more than four decades, the Phantom II was flown by a dozen nations. In the United States it became the essential mission aircraft for the Air Force, Navy and Marines. Pilots liked its performance

so much that the F-4 was selected as the official aircraft for both the Navy Blue Angels and the Air Force Thunderbirds, the armed services' aerobatic flight-demonstration teams.

Although most F-4s served with the Air Force, it was a Navy initiative that first pursued McDonnell's ideas. Naval planners wanted a carrier-based supersonic interceptor that could cruise to a radius of 250 nautical miles, remain on station for about three hours and destroy any intruding aircraft necessary.

McDonnell proposed a plane that could climb straight up after takeoff and attack intruders at speeds up to Mach 2—twice the speed of sound—with Sparrow missiles instead of machine guns.

The Navy responded in July 1955 by signing a letter of intent to purchase two prototypes, to be configured as two-place, all-weather, fleet air-defense aircraft.

The F4H-1 made its first flight on May 27, 1958, and almost immediately experienced hydraulic-system malfunctions. "The flight only lasted about 21 minutes. Just long enough for me to learn how to fly the aircraft so I could land it," test pilot Bob Little recalled on the 40th anniversary of that flight. "But on the fourth flight, we got a real taste of the aircraft's performance, and I knew we had a winner. We lit up the afterburners and, in no time, we were at Mach 1.8 and 50,000 ft. It outclassed anything I had ever flown up until that time, and I knew there was nothing that could touch it." In honor of McDonnell's FH-1 Phantom, the company's first jet fighter and the first carrier-based combat jet aircraft in the world, the new plane was called the Phantom II.

Navy squadrons were first equipped with F4H-1s in October 1961. Impressed with the plane's performance, the Air Force took the unusual step the following January of testing an aircraft first designed for sea operation. Six months later, in June 1962, the U.S. Marine Corps got in on the act and took delivery of its first Phantom II—designated the F-4 across the military spectrum that September. Seventeen years later, on Oct. 25, 1979, the Air Force took delivery of Phantom No. 5057, the last F-4 manu-

The Navy's flight-performance team, the Blue Angels—flying, above, in a delta formation—and its Air Force counterpart, the Thunderbirds, both adopted the F-4 as their demonstration jet of choice in the late '60s and early '70s.

factured in the U.S., for use by the air force of the Republic of Korea. Another 138 Phantoms were built in Japan, completing the largest production run for any U.S.-designed supersonic fighter.

The F-4 distinguished itself in combat from Vietnam to the Gulf. Over the years the Phantom evolved through 20 specific models to incorporate more powerful engines—the F-4E's J79-GE-17 turbojets produced a total of 35,800 pounds of thrust with afterburners—deadlier weapons and improved avionics. Its most significant changes, perhaps, were those connected to the F-4G "Wild Weasel," in which a plane intended to protect aircraft carriers was adapted to fight the most difficult land missions, attacking ground-based air-defense systems. After retiring the legendary fighters from active duty, the Air Force would later call its F-4Cs the "most effective fighter of the '60s." The Navy would remember the Phantom as its "finest air weapon."

VITALS	
Designation	F-4E Phantom II
Wingspan	38 ft. 5 in.
Length	63 ft.
Max. Weight	61,795 pounds
Top Speed	1485 mph
Cruising Speed	590 mph
Range	1612 miles
Ceiling	58,750 ft.

The F-15A at right isn't shy about showing off its lethal belly; the Eagle's weapons capability includes AIM-7 Sparrow missiles, AIM-9 Sidewinder missiles, plus 16,000 pounds of mixed ordnance and an internal 20mm M-61A1 Vulcan cannon.

F-15
Eagle

• McDonnell Douglas

Combining maneuverability with lightning-fast acceleration, the Eagle remains one of the most feared tactical fighters in the world.

Although the Air Force had begun design studies in the mid-1960s on a plane to succeed the McDonnell F-4 Phantom, that fighter's stellar success in Vietnam squelched any sense of urgency for a replacement. This complacency changed suddenly in the late 1960s when satellite photos revealed that the Soviets might have leapfrogged the U.S. Air Force with the development of two high-performance aircraft, the MiG-23 and MiG-25. Mindful of the way MiG-15s had so quickly rendered F-80 Shooting Stars obsolete in Korea, the development of a new air-superiority fighter was given a high priority, with three contractors competing to build a plane simply identified as the "FX."

McDonnell Douglas won the contest. Paying due respect to the lessons learned in Vietnam about air combat in extremely tight quarters, it designed a highly maneuverable single-seat aircraft that would allow the pilot to launch a missile at its enemy then rapidly turn away. An aircraft's responsiveness is chiefly determined by two factors. The first is the plane's thrust-to-weight ratio. Simply put, more power is better. The second is wing loading—the weight borne by each square foot of wing—and lighter wing loading makes for a more maneuverable aircraft. McDonnell Douglas offered a design for the FX that incorporated high-thrust engines and a large, 608-sq.-ft. wing. The resulting plane was the F-15 Eagle.

The first F-15 flew on July 27, 1972. Its two-year shakedown period proceeded flawlessly without the loss of a life, an aircraft or serious damage to either. This new aircraft won instant acceptance from its pilots. Its advanced avionics provided a battle-management system that represented the merger of computer technology with radar: Critical information about electronically identified bogeys is projected on a "head-up" display on the cockpit's windscreen so that the pilot need not look down to track and destroy targets.

To minimize refueling on long missions, the F-15 could be fit with conformable fuel tanks that extended the plane's range without denying precious wing space to its weapons capability.

Although originally designed as an all-weather air-superiority fighter, the superlative performance of the F-15 suggested it might serve as a bomber as well. In 1987, a new variation appeared, the F-15E Strike Eagle, sporting two Pratt & Whitney turbofan engines capable of 58,000 pounds of thrust with afterburners and a seat added behind the pilot for a Weapons Systems Operator (WSO). The WSO (pronounced wiz-o) controls a variety of radar-, laser- and infrared-guided smart bombs via a sophisticated electronic tactical-warfare system capable of jamming both long-range search radar and short-range surface-to-air missile-guidance systems while the F-15 intercepts targets.

Three NATO F-15s patrol arctic waters off the coast of Norway. The F-15's all-weather capability makes it an attractive plane to air forces around the world. Israel, Japan, and Saudi Arabia have all added some variation of the Eagle to their airborne arsenals.

These innovations made for a truly dominant warplane: According to the Federation of American Scientists, the F-15C has achieved an unheard of 95-0 kill ratio in all its combat engagements for the USAF and other friendly air forces, making it the most lethal fighter in the sky.

Electronics, however, which provide both the air-superiority and ground-attack versions of the F-15 Eagle with their outstanding capabilities, are also their greatest weakness: The Eagle's original systems predate the global proliferation of the microprocessor and have reached the limits of modernization—in other words, the Eagle's technological potential has partially "landed." To combat this obsolescence, some 526 Eagles, less than half of the more than 1200 built, have been either retrofitted with replacement avionics suites or have rolled off the assembly line with newer technologies already installed.

A replacement for the F-15, the Lockheed Martin F-22 Raptor, has been designed and is now undergoing flight tests. Whether it becomes operational depends largely on the geopolitical climate. The collapse of the Soviet Union lowers the possibility that a confrontation between an F-15 and a Sukhoi Su-35 or Su-37, Russia's premier line of fighters, might ever occur; the Eagle, therefore, may retain its supremacy in the skies for years, perhaps decades, to come.

VITALS	
Designation	F-15C Eagle
Wingspan	42 ft. 9¾ in.
Length	63 ft. 9 in.
Max. Weight	68,000 pounds
Top Speed	Over 1600 mph
Cruising Speed	570 mph
Range	2500 miles with external fuel tanks
Ceiling	65,000 ft.

The svelte and sexy **F-16** below bares its varied fangs—a wide array of air-to-air and air-to-ground supersonic rockets. With its multi-platform capabilities and a relatively affordable price tag, the Fighting Falcon is a popular choice for national air defense around the world.

F-16
Fighting Falcon

• General Dynamics

Arguably the most versatile fighter in the sky pound for pound, the F-16 flew more sorties in the Gulf War than any other aircraft.

The F-16 Fighting Falcon provides a glimpse of the future of combat aviation. It also bucks the trend of heavier, more mechanically complex and increasingly expensive aircraft that began with the Republic P-47 Thunderbolt in 1942.

In the early 1970s the U.S. Air Force created the Lightweight Fighter Program to see if defense contractors could draw on new technologies to produce a leaner and cheaper fighter. From the major proposals, two prototypes were built. General Dynamics, since absorbed into Lockheed Martin, won the contract to build its single-engine design, designated the YF-16. And Northrop was asked to build a twin-engine fighter, the YF-17. (A "Y" pre-

fix means an aircraft is built for service tests, with the anticipation of being put into production.)

The General Dynamics single-engine single-seat F-16, which flew for the first time on January 20, 1974, won the competition with a design that incorporated several bold ideas. The most visible innovation is the body of the plane itself, in which the fuselage is blended into the wing. This integrated design makes the F-16 so strong that even with a full load of fuel it can withstand up to nine G's (nine times the force of gravity)—more than any current production fighter. Another noticeable feature is the F-16's bubble canopy, which greatly improves the pilot's sight-

VITALS	
Designation	F-16C Fighting Falcon
Wingspan	32 ft. 10 in.
Length	47 ft. 8 in.
Max. Weight	42,500 pounds
Top Speed	1500 mph
Cruising Speed	577 mph
Range	2415 miles with external fuel tanks
Ceiling	50,000 ft.

line. The most significant innovation, however, which *cannot* be seen from outside the plane, is the "fly-by-wire" system of electric wiring that replaces the network of cables and linkages used on older aircraft. In addition to simplifying the construction of the aircraft, fly-by-wire technology also makes it possible to relocate the stick from its tradition position between the pilot's knees to a more comfortable position at his side, providing ease of movement during high G-force maneuvers. Accordingly, the F-16's seat is raked back from the usual 13 degrees to a more reclined 30 degrees so that its occupant can withstand such high gravitational pull. A highly accurate inertial navigation system, coupled to a computer, provides heading and steering information.

The F-16 also incorporates one of the most important lessons designers learned from their experience with the F-15. While electronic components may continue to get smaller, complete avionics systems only grow larger. To meet still unanticipated needs, the Fighting Falcon was built to easily accommodate the expansion of its avionics suite.

Perhaps the most unusual aspect of the plane's construction is where it is built. Component manufacturing is shared by the Unites States and four of its NATO allies: Belgium, Denmark, the Netherlands and Norway. (In the future, components will also be manufactured in Spain.) Airframe assembly lines are in the Netherlands and Belgium, where final assembly of the 25,000-pound-thrust Pratt & Whitney engine also takes place. Some Fighting Falcons are equipped with a comparable General Electric F110 turbofan.

Because the F-16 is a relatively lightweight plane, it can be powered by a single engine and still carry 12,000 pounds of ordnance. A typical weapons load may include gravity bombs, air-to-air rockets and laser-guided munitions. An internally mounted 20mm cannon permits close-range engagement. The F-16 first achieved combat-ready status in October 1980; during the Gulf War, this flexibility led to the F-16's use in more sorties than any other aircraft. Its targets included radar sites, tanks and airfields.

The $34.3 million Fighting Falcon is neither the fastest nor the most powerful multipurpose fighter. What it offers, however, is a balance of military capability and economic value that is likely to keep it a popular choice among air forces around the world well into the 21st century.

A Fighting Falcon (above) deployed its full load of low-drag MK 84 "dumb" bombs during a 1990 training run. "Hauling iron"—or the air-to-ground attack—is the F-16's bread-and-butter mission and presents a demanding challenge to its pilots.

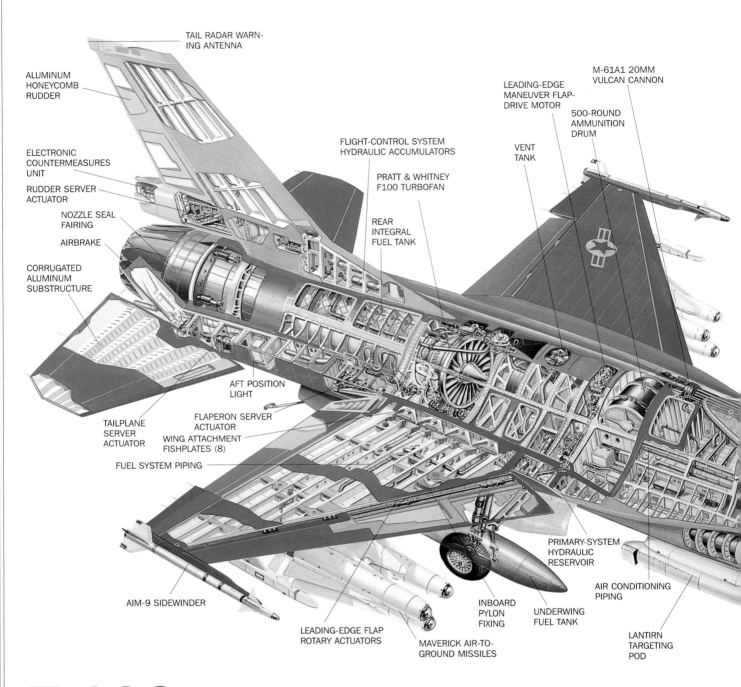

TAIL RADAR WARN-
ING ANTENNA

ALUMINUM
HONEYCOMB
RUDDER

ELECTRONIC
COUNTERMEASURES
UNIT

RUDDER SERVER
ACTUATOR

NOZZLE SEAL
FAIRING

AIRBRAKE

CORRUGATED
ALUMINUM
SUBSTRUCTURE

TAILPLANE
SERVER
ACTUATOR

AFT POSITION
LIGHT

FLAPERON SERVER
ACTUATOR

WING ATTACHMENT
FISHPLATES (8)

FUEL SYSTEM PIPING

AIM-9 SIDEWINDER

LEADING-EDGE FLAP
ROTARY ACTUATORS

MAVERICK AIR-TO-
GROUND MISSILES

INBOARD
PYLON
FIXING

UNDERWING
FUEL TANK

PRIMARY-SYSTEM
HYDRAULIC
RESERVOIR

AIR CONDITIONING
PIPING

LANTIRN
TARGETING
POD

FLIGHT-CONTROL SYSTEM
HYDRAULIC ACCUMULATORS

PRATT & WHITNEY
F100 TURBOFAN

REAR
INTEGRAL
FUEL TANK

LEADING-EDGE
MANEUVER FLAP-
DRIVE MOTOR

M-61A1 20MM
VULCAN CANNON

500-ROUND
AMMUNITION
DRUM

VENT
TANK

F-16C
Fighting Falcon

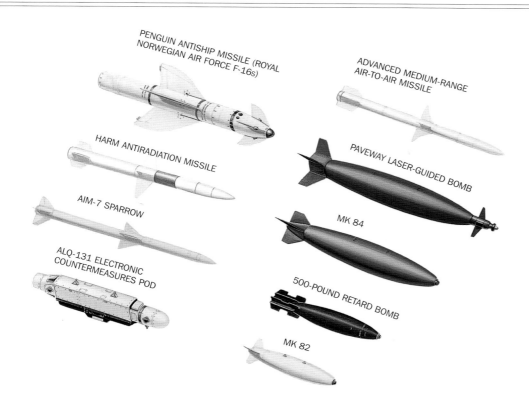

PENGUIN ANTISHIP MISSILE (ROYAL NORWEGIAN AIR FORCE F-16s)

ADVANCED MEDIUM-RANGE AIR-TO-AIR MISSILE

HARM ANTIRADIATION MISSILE

PAVEWAY LASER-GUIDED BOMB

AIM-7 SPARROW

MK 84

ALQ-131 ELECTRONIC COUNTERMEASURES POD

500-POUND RETARD BOMB

MK 82

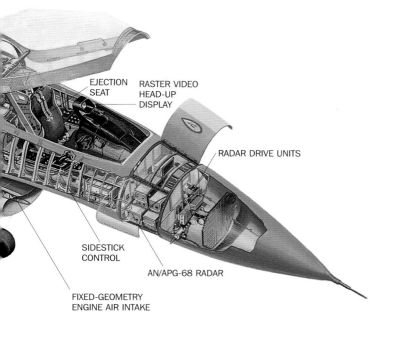

EJECTION SEAT

RASTER VIDEO HEAD-UP DISPLAY

RADAR DRIVE UNITS

SIDESTICK CONTROL

AN/APG-68 RADAR

FIXED-GEOMETRY ENGINE AIR INTAKE

EJECTION SEATS

Learning to pilot any plane requires skill. Learning to fly a high-performance jet, however, requires literally hundreds of hours in the cockpit of a multi-million dollar aircraft. Saving pilots is more than a humanitarian gesture—it is also good economics.

The need for a quick-escape mechanism emerged in World War II. Germany was the first to install ejection seats in aircraft, first employing a blast of compressed air and, later, an explosive charge, the method still in use today. Those seats saved the lives of about 60 German combat fliers.

In the United States, Sgt. Lawrence Lambert became the first American to successfully eject, during an experiment on August 17, 1947, in which he blasted out of a P-61. As planes traveled faster, however, ejection seat design became a deadly balancing act. The explosive force had to be sufficient, without killing or crippling the pilot, to thrust the seat through the canopy of the cockpit and also clear the tail structure.

Today, F-15s, F-16s and F-117s use the Advanced Concept Ejection Seat, which permits a safe ejection even from a plane parked on the ground. During low-altitude ejection, small gyroscope-controlled rockets stabilize the seat. Regardless of the improvements, ejection almost always produces some degree of injury, ranging from black eyes and bruised ribs to more serious injury, including broken bones and spinal damage.

The F-117A Nighthawk (below) sports a futuristic design that looks more at home in a George Lucas movie than in the Air Force's 49th Fighter Wing. Its price tag—a cool $122 million—reflects the considerable labor that went into creating 65 ft. of state-of-the-art avionics and integrated stealth technology.

F-117
Nighthawk

• Lockheed

Nearly invisible to radar and infrared sensors, the so-called stealth fighter has ushered in a brave new world of combat aircraft.

With the Lockheed F-117 Nighthawk, the U.S. Air Force achieved the "impossible dream" of building a virtually invisible airplane. The distinctively shaped plane is, of course, quite visible to the eye. But to the "eyes" of the radar anti-aircraft systems that peer through the night sky and cloud cover, the twin-engine jet is virtually invisible— that is, until the moment it opens its bomb-bay doors and unleashes its complement of laser-targeted and laser-guided missiles.

The F-117 works on a simple theory that is extremely difficult and very expensive to execute. Like light waves, radar waves can be made to reflect at angles away from their point of origin. The greater the amount of energy that a target dissipates or absorbs, the less that is available to reflect back to a radar receiver. Much of the energy impinging upon the Nighthawk's unusual shape is deflected at oblique angles, and some of the energy is actually trapped by the F-117's radar-absorbent skin. The result is that the Nighthawk (and the Northrop B-2 Spirit, which was built with similar technology) returns the radar cross-section of a large bird. Embedding the aircraft's two relatively low-power non-afterburning General Electric engines—which generate a combined thrust of

21,200 pounds—inside its airframe, surrounding them with heat-shielding tiles like those on the space shuttles, and mixing the hot engine exhaust with the frigid ambient air encountered at high altitude makes the F-117 as invisible to infrared sensors as it is to radar. In friendly skies, the F-117 navigates with standard military avionics. In combat, however, it relies upon passive sensors. Because radar use would give away the F-117's presence, it requires a more complex inertial navigation system than other military aircraft.

A proof-of-concept model for the F-117, code-named Have Blue, was built at the Lockheed Skunk Works in California in the mid-1970s. It flew over Groom Dry Lake Bed, Nevada, popularly known as "Area 51," in 1977. A development program ensued, with the Nighthawk completing its first flight in 1981. Production began the following year and continued until 1990. About 54 Nighthawks are believed to be operational, 36 of which are believed to be combat ready.

To help conceal the project, many of its components were literally taken off the shelf, from the spare-parts supplies of other military aircraft. The Nighthawk's landing gear, for example, consists of the nose gear of a Fairchild A-10 Thunderbolt and the main gear of an F-15 Eagle. The fly-by-wire

The single-seat multipurpose stealth fighter (above, with weapons-bay doors open) was the only coalition aircraft to strike targets within Baghdad's city limits during the Gulf War. The Nighthawk's typical munitions complement is two 2000-pound GBU-27 laser-guided bombs.

computer from an F-16 Fighting Falcon operates the stealthy fighter's control surfaces. The pilot of a Nighthawk sits in a standard ACES ejection seat and looks at the same cockpit display naval aviators rely on while flying McDonnell Douglas F/A-18 Hornets.

An F-117-equipped unit, the 4450th Tactical Group, became operational in October 1983. The high-tech fighter's first known combat mission occurred six years later, when two Nighthawks attacked the Rio Hato barracks during Operation Just Cause, the U.S. invasion of Panama. In 1991, 36 Nighthawks were deployed to the Gulf War, where they flew nightly missions into downtown Baghdad, attacking power stations, command centers and other high-value targets.

The era of the Nighthawk's seeming invincibility ended on March 27, 1999, however: An F-117 supporting NATO operations in the former Yugoslavia was downed by enemy fire. Whether it was a lucky shot or the result of "chaining" several distant radar stations to detect the Nighthawk's tiny signature is a moot point. Although the pilot survived and was rescued by U.S. forces, his $122-million aircraft and some of its secret stealth technology is believed to have been captured intact.

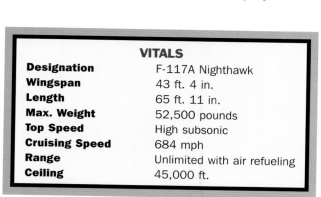

VITALS

Designation	F-117A Nighthawk
Wingspan	43 ft. 4 in.
Length	65 ft. 11 in.
Max. Weight	52,500 pounds
Top Speed	High subsonic
Cruising Speed	684 mph
Range	Unlimited with air refueling
Ceiling	45,000 ft.

CHAPTER 4
Attack Aircraft

A-10 Thunderbolt II, 1991

Two A-7E Corsair IIs (left) from Attack Squadron 72 of Carrier Air Wing 7 soared over the aircraft carrier *USS Dwight D. Eisenhower* during a mission in the Mediterranean Sea in 1989. The AC-130 Spectre (above) has served the U.S. Air Force as a side-firing gunship since the late 1960s. The latest model, the AC-130U Spooky, packs a 25mm Gatling gun, a 40mm cannon and a 105mm Howitzer.

Attack Aircraft

Known more for firepower—spraying thousands of rounds per minute on their unfortunate targets—than aesthetics, these bulky yet deadly aircraft are the Grim Reapers of the skies.

The designation "attack" aircraft does not so much identify a particular type of airplane as it does describe the specific combat mission of firing at targets on the ground while flying at low altitude. Under this definition, the unofficial birth of the attack aircraft took place in New York on August 20, 1910, over a race track in Sheepshead Bay, Brooklyn. Flying as a passenger in a Curtiss biplane, U.S. Army Lt. Jacob E. Fickel shot his Springfield .30-'03 rifle at a roughly 3-ft.-sq. target, scoring two hits. As was the case with most early attempts to use the airplane as a weapons platform, the Army was not impressed. When the

Signals Corps had acquired its own Wright Flyers the previous year, the Army's plans for its aircraft were limited to observation missions. Despite Fickel's marksmanship, the Army issued its fliers binoculars and not rifles.

The passive use of aircraft as observation platforms changed rapidly in the opening weeks of World War I, as rival pilots and their passengers began firing at Zeppelins, dropping crude bombs on enemy positions and, in short order, attacking each other. Within a matter of months aircraft designs diverged according to mission. Bombers destined to fly strategic missions were optimized

Northrop A-17s were the last of the interwar single-engine attack planes; five machine guns and a capacity for two dozen bombs made the A-17 more heavily armed than the pursuit planes of the day.

A Douglas A-4 Skyhawk (above) strained at its catapult moments before streaking off the deck of an aircraft carrier during the Vietnam War. These light-attack bombers—dubbed "Heinemann's Hot Rod" in honor of Douglas designer Ed Heinemann—were initiated into combat during the U.S. Navy's first carrier-launched raid against North Vietnam in early August 1964.

for carrying heavier loads, flying farther and eventually flying higher. Fighters, which Americans insisted upon calling pursuit planes, evolved as scout aircraft and were equipped with machine guns and steel-edge plates or timing mechanisms to protect their propellers. A distinct class of aircraft designed to attack troops on the ground would not emerge until the 1920s. And it would not be until Germany began to regain its military footing in the 1930s that aviation would see the introduction of effective dive-bombers and, during World War II, planes optimized for destroying tanks and other armored vehicles.

When the United States entered World War II, its best attack aircraft was the Douglas A-20 Havoc. It was from this plane that American servicemen would stage their first low-altitude daytime bomb runs, on Dutch airfields. During the war a replacement for the A-20, the Douglas A-26 Invader, went into production. After the war the fate of this light bomber underscored the uncer-

tain attitude of the newly formed U.S. Air Force toward attack aircraft per se.

In 1948, soon after its creation as a distinct armed service on equal footing with the Army and Navy, the Air Force dropped the "attack" designation altogether. Thus, the A-26 became the B-26 bomber, which staged successful nighttime ground attacks on supply lines in Korea. In 1966, however, the Air Force resurrected the A designation ostensibly to circumvent the Thai government, which had banned U.S. bombers from its bases. Called an attack aircraft for convenience, the A-26A was assigned to Special Forces operations in Southeast Asia and though the aircraft's basic mission would never change, the Air Force's view of attack aircraft soon would.

During the Cold War, the Air Force had come to perceive its primary mission as maintaining the bomber and missile forces that formed, along with submarine-based missiles, America's nuclear triad, which held the Soviet Union in check through the threat of assured mutual destruction. That equation had relegated ground attack to a secondary mission for fighters and bombers—a situation that would no longer pass muster in the Vietnam War.

Much of the dilemma rested on the service's new choice for the attack role, the Vought A-7D Corsair II, an adapted Navy attack-bomber. Modified for the types of ground-attack missions flown in Korea, the military did not think to question its potential usefulness in Vietnam. Capable though the Corsair might have been, it ultimately proved unsuitable for fighting a guerrilla war under a jungle canopy—A-7s simply could not perform well at low speeds and in tightly confined locations. The Air Force soon came to the realization it needed specialized attack airplanes for these new battlefields.

Some alternatives already existed, in the form of modified C-47 and C-130 cargo planes. Armed with 7.62mm General Electric SUU-11A mini-guns capable of firing 6000 rounds per minute, they became the AC-47 and AC-130 gunships that deprived the Viet Cong of their best firing positions and defended South Vietnamese hamlets.

The Air Force's first pure ground-attack aircraft, the Fairchild A-10 Thunderbolt II, would be the end result of the ground-attack question in Vietnam. While not available before the end of that war, the sturdy A-10 "Warthog" would fight in the Persian Gulf War and, later, in the American-led NATO effort to dislodge Serbian forces from Kosovo in 1999.

As the A-10 approaches the end of its life cycle, the future of the pure-attack aircraft appears about to be eclipsed by a new class of aircraft, the Joint Strike Fighter (JSF). Now undergoing flight tests, the JSF will provide all three services with a common airframe capable of carrying out virtually every mission short of strategic bombing, the task of the Northrop B-2 Spirit, and total air dominance, the role defined for the new Lockheed Martin F-22 Raptor.

An A-10 Thunderbolt (above) cruised in camouflage colors over Bosnia. The first A-10s based overseas were assigned to the 81st Tactical Fighter Wing based at RAF Bentwaters and RAF Woodbridge. With 108 aircraft in its command, the 81st TFW's primary purpose was to support NATO forces against the threat of possible enemy armored invasions throughout regions of Europe.

Two U.S. Air Force A-10 Thunderbolts, more commonly called Warthogs, plowed single-file through wispy clouds en route to targets in the former Yugoslavia during NATO's Operation Allied Force on April 22, 1999.

An A-20G over Germany in 1945 (above) plunged earthward, its bomb-bay doors open and .50-cal. turret machine guns at the ready. Like some G models, this aircraft also carried 500-pound bombs on its wings. A member of the extended A-20 family was part of every major Allied air force, although American A-20 crews did not see much action in Europe until the preinvasion buildup of 1944.

A-20
Havoc

• **Douglas**

A jack-of-all-trades warplane, the A-20 Havoc reinvented itself perhaps more times than any combat aircraft before or since.

Few aircraft have undergone as many dramatic transformations as the Douglas A-20 Havoc, the chief attack aircraft during the opening months of World War II. Designed as a high-altitude bomber, the A-20 was used as a medium-altitude bomber and low-flying attack aircraft. Later, A-20s would be converted into troop transports and test aircraft for experimental technologies. More than 6000 would be built in seven production models.

The A-20 originated in 1936 as a Douglas Aircraft high-altitude bomber, the Model 7B. The

first prototype flew in October 1938, and while the U.S. Army was interested, it had no money to build a fleet; in fact, at the time the Army had only 300 pilots. France and Belgium pounced at the opportunity to buy the plane, designated the DB-7, but fewer than 70 arrived before France fell to Hitler's Blitz. Britain's Royal Air Force bought the remainder of the order and converted the aircraft into night fighters, intruder fighters and trainers.

With Europe at war a steady stream of new weapons began to flow in the United States. The

VITALS	
Designation	A-20G Havoc
Wingspan	61 ft. 4 in.
Length	48 ft.
Gross Weight	24,125 pounds
Top Speed	317 mph
Cruising Speed	256 mph
Range	2100 miles
Ceiling	23,700 ft.

Army ordered 63 modified 7Bs, designating them the A-20 Havoc. As production was about to ramp up, the Army realized that what its arsenal really lacked was not a high-altitude light-attack bomber but a lower-altitude heavy-attack aircraft. As a result, only one A-20 was built with the turbo-supercharged engine needed for high-altitude flight. This plane would be redesignated the XP-70 and, with new engines, become the proto-type for the Douglas P-70, the interim night fighter that served until the introduction of the Northrop P-61 Black Widow in 1943.

A production model, the Douglas A-20A, made its maiden flight September 16, 1940. Powered by a pair of 1600-hp Wright engines, it could carry 1600 pounds of bombs and seven .30-cal. machine guns—four forward-firing attack guns, two defensive guns in a rear cockpit and one in the belly. The plane required a four-man crew: a pilot, a navigator, a bombardier and a gunner. Only 143 A-20As were built before the Army decided the Allies needed something similar. In October 1940 the Army Air Corps ordered 999 Douglas A-20Bs—with a "greenhouse" stepped-edge nose for the bombardier that harkened back to earlier DB-7 designs—and sent more than 600 of them to Russia under Lend-Lease.

With the Douglas A-20C, the Army went back to the basic A-20A airframe, augmenting it with armor plating and self-sealing fuel tanks to protect the crew; it also had improved Wright engines. The original plan was to ship these aircraft to the RAF and the Soviet air force; however, many were swiftly reassigned to the U.S. Army Air Corps when the United States entered the war.

The Douglas A-20G Havoc became the next, and eventually the largest, production version. Upgrades included four 20mm cannons, which often jammed and were later traded in for six .50-cal. machine guns, and larger air filters for hot-weather engine cooling. The last production "block" of the A20-G series had wings strong enough to carry four 500-pound bombs, which increased the Havoc's total bomb load to 4000 pounds. A later A-20H model eked an extra 200 hp from two Wright R-2600-29 engines.

Havocs flew tactical bombing missions in Europe and in the Pacific and were especially effective in low-altitude attack missions against airfields and shipping. Beginning in November 1944 they were replaced by the Douglas A-26 Invader, a more powerful aircraft optimized for mid-level bombing, ground strafing and rocket attacks. Although removed from combat, Havocs were not abandoned entirely. Some would be reconfigured as reconnaissance aircraft, and a few were used to test radical ideas of the day, including jet booster engines for short-field takeoffs and, less successfully, tracked gear instead of wheels for landing on ice and mud. Most of the versatile A-20s, however, were converted into CA-20 transports, and some of these would remain in service into the 1960s.

A squadron of Douglas A-20s (above) dropped tidy, single-file columns of bombs near Shreveport, Louisiana, during war games in 1941. During the Pacific war, Havocs specialized in low-level attacks that targeted Japanese shipping and airfields.

A-7
Corsair II

• Vought

A move by the Navy to save money gives birth to a line of ground-breaking aircraft and prompts the Air Force to get in on the act, too.

Politics has always played a role in the selection of military weapons; their production means local jobs and prosperity. By the early 1960s, competition in the aerospace industry had become so intense that political savvy was as important a requirement for winning aircraft contracts as technical expertise. The genesis of the A-7 Corsair II illustrates the point. As jet engines grew more efficient and reliable, the Navy realized the improvements could be leveraged to protect its carrier force since planes with greater range allow aircraft carriers to be stationed farther at sea from hostile

areas, affording the massive ships more time to detect and respond to attacks.

In the early 1960s the Navy calculated that the least expensive way to achieve this objective would be to create a hybrid aircraft. The front-running proposal envisioned mating a new, powerful Pratt & Whitney TF-30 turbofan—already slated for a new supersonic fighter, the F-111—to a modified airframe from the Douglas A-4 Skyhawk, the Navy's premier attack aircraft at the time. When Vought Aircraft Company learned of the Navy's plan, it launched a major lobbying effort to convince the

An A-7E (above) based aboard the carrier *USS John F. Kennedy* in the Red Sea, brought naval greetings to Saddam Hussein's forces in February 1991, in the form of eight MK 82 500-pound bombs. Just for good measure, an air-to-air AIM-9 Sidewinder missile was tucked under its cheek-position point, an insurance policy against encounters with airborne unfriendlies.

Pentagon to first order an industry-wide competition for a new class of aircraft, the Light Navy Attack Bomber. Douglas, Grumman, Vought and North American submitted designs, and in February 1964 the Navy selected Vought's proposal, ordering six planes for evaluation.

Vought, however, faced several contractual limitations. The engineering director, Sol Love, knowingly incurred a penalty by approving a wing design that carried the project over a specified weight limit by 600 pounds. That $750,000 fine would later pay off.

When it rolled out for its first flight in September 1965, the stubby-nosed Corsair looked like a chunky version of the Vought F-8 Crusader supersonic fighter. The single-seat A-7 had one Pratt & Whitney TF-30P6 nonafterburning engine fitted aft, with a distinctive gaping chin intake that dominated the lower half of the fuselage. Built in near record time, the first A-7 was delivered in September 1966. Corsairs entered combat in Vietnam in December 1967, and the A-7 went on to achieve the lowest loss rate of any warplane flown there.

In a fundamental sense, the 1545 A-7 airframes produced represented four very different airplanes. The A-7A, B and C versions differed only in terms of engine updates and minor modifications. The A-7D was designed for the Air Force, which specified more than 20 changes including a 20mm Vulcan cannon and the receptacle-refueling system. Like the A-7D, the Navy's upgraded model, the

The "artistic" stencils on an A-7E (above) reflected the number of sorties the pilot had flown during Operation Desert Storm and the number of general-purpose bombs, cluster bombs and antiradiation missiles he dropped or fired.

A-7E, was given a major propulsion upgrade through a joint Rolls-Royce/Alison TF-41-series engine but retained a design consistent with carrier-based flight. Both of these later Corsairs pioneered a sophisticated avionics suite—a head-up display, central navigation-weapon delivery computer and projected-map display—that became the standard for modern warplanes. A final version built for the Air Force, the YA-7F, was modified for supersonic flight.

Love's choice to absorb the $750,000 design penalty would indeed evolve into a lucrative investment. As warplanes age, they tend to gain weight from the addition of new weapons. The Corsair's stronger wing meant that instead of ordering an entirely new type of aircraft to accommodate heavier weapons, the Air Force and Navy could simply continue to fly the A-7s—whose wing pylons could carry virtually every type of droppable weapon—that were rolling out of the Vought factories. As in any other manufacturing operation, the first product off an assembly line is the most expensive, the last the most profitable. With the eventual capacity of 20,000 pounds of weapons, versus the 2000 pounds of the old Douglas A-20 Havoc, the A-7 became one of the most cost-effective aircraft ever built.

From Vietnam to the Persian Gulf, the A-7 would be part of every significant U.S. military action. Although its American career is over, it remains in use in at least three foreign air forces.

VITALS	
Designation	A-7D Corsair II
Wingspan	38 ft. 8 in.
Length	46 ft.
Max. Weight	42,000 pounds
Top Speed	660 mph
Cruising Speed	653 mph
Range	3075 miles
Ceiling	37,200 ft.

Against a cloudscape, the weapons capabilities of the A-10 (above) are clearly visible. In addition to a lethal seven-barrel 30mm Avenger cannon, the Warthog can deliver up to 16,000 pounds of mixed ordnance. It was ready for combat in 1978.

A-10
Thunderbolt II

• Fairchild

With a fistful of missiles and a tank-shredding cannon, the A-10 gives grateful ground forces a new definition of close air-support.

Vietnam taught the Pentagon that detailed analyses of its historic battles offered little guidance on fighting a determined enemy in jungle terrain. One result was that the U.S. Air Force would, at long last, be given the resources to build a specialized ground-attack aircraft. Technically, the Air Force had assumed the responsibility of developing ground-attack aircraft in 1947, when it was created as a separate branch of the military. Largely for budgetary reasons, however, it concentrated its air-

craft development dollars on strategic bombers to carry nuclear weapons against Soviet targets and fighters to protect those bombers. In the late 1960s the Air Force had satisfied its requirement for a ground-attack aircraft with the Vought A-7D Corsair II. The Corsair, however, had been built to reflect the close air-support mandate required in the Korean conflict: arrive fast and hit with accuracy. The guerrilla war in the jungles of Vietnam, however, added a new angle to the close air-support

VITALS	
Designation	A-10A Thunderbolt II
Wingspan	57 ft. 6 in.
Length	53 ft. 4 in.
Gross Weight	47,000 pounds
Top Speed	450 mph
Cruising Speed	335 mph
Range	800 miles
Ceiling	44,200 ft.

mission: An attack aircraft now had to be highly maneuverable at low speeds and low altitude. What the Air Force wished for, in essence, was a heavily armed, armored crop duster.

The solution came in the form of a seemingly indestructible and notably ugly airplane, the Fairchild A-10 Thunderbolt II, better known as the "Warthog." The single-seater's most distinctive feature is the placement of its two massive General Electric TF34-GE-100 turbofans—9000 pounds of thrust each—placed high on the fuselage, well aft of the cockpit. What looks odd in profile is essential to the plane's survival rate: The engines' unusual positioning makes them less vulnerable to damage from foreign objects that might be swept into their intakes and somewhat protected, by the plane's wings, against ground-based small arms.

Other protective features of the A-10 include self-sealing fuel tanks (insulated by internal and external foam) and a titanium "bathtub" that protects the cockpit and has been tested favorably against 23mm armor-piercing projectiles. Titanium shielding also protects critical control areas, and flight-control systems are triple redundant with a manual backup. The durable plane is able to fly with one engine inoperable

and can stay aloft with one of its twin tail structures missing. When it lands, repairs can be quickly made in the field, as engines, vertical stabilizers and many of the other parts are interchangeable left to right. An on-board auxiliary power unit even compresses air so the jets have self-starting capability.

In addition to protecting the pilot and engines, the unique design makes the A-10 the near-perfect weapons platform for close air-support operations. Its wings and fuselage have 11 weapon-attachment points for an assortment of 16,000 pounds of bombs and missiles, and its 30mm GAU-8A Gatling gun can spit out a withering 3900 rounds per minute. An upgrade program equipped A-10 pilots with infrared sensors and goggles for night fighting.

Although clearly technically superior to the Vought A-7D Corsair II, the Air Force faced a stiff political battle to win acceptance for the Fairchild A-10 Thunderbolt II. At the insistence of Congress the A-7 and A-10 were forced to compete in a fly-off contest. Even though the A-10 flew without its cannon or principal missile—the AGM-65 Maverick—

(continued)

An A-10 (above) sat on a Saudi runway in September 1990, part of the multinational force assembling against Iraqi aggression in the Persian Gulf. Four days into the air war, two Warthogs provided critical support during a successful rescue mission deep in Iraqi territory, destroying an enemy truck seconds before it reached a downed U.S. Navy aircrewman.

A-10A Thunderbolt II

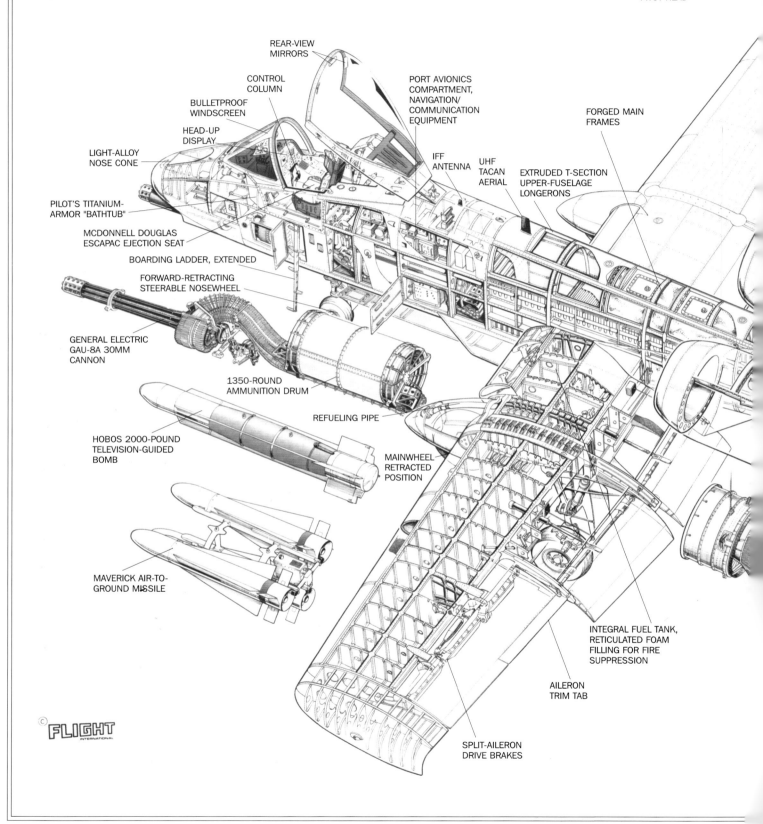

PITOT HEAD

REAR-VIEW MIRRORS

CONTROL COLUMN

PORT AVIONICS COMPARTMENT, NAVIGATION/ COMMUNICATION EQUIPMENT

BULLETPROOF WINDSCREEN

FORGED MAIN FRAMES

HEAD-UP DISPLAY

IFF ANTENNA

LIGHT-ALLOY NOSE CONE

UHF TACAN AERIAL

EXTRUDED T-SECTION UPPER-FUSELAGE LONGERONS

PILOT'S TITANIUM-ARMOR "BATHTUB"

MCDONNELL DOUGLAS ESCAPAC EJECTION SEAT

BOARDING LADDER, EXTENDED

FORWARD-RETRACTING STEERABLE NOSEWHEEL

GENERAL ELECTRIC GAU-8A 30MM CANNON

1350-ROUND AMMUNITION DRUM

REFUELING PIPE

HOBOS 2000-POUND TELEVISION-GUIDED BOMB

MAINWHEEL RETRACTED POSITION

MAVERICK AIR-TO-GROUND MISSILE

INTEGRAL FUEL TANK, RETICULATED FOAM FILLING FOR FIRE SUPPRESSION

AILERON TRIM TAB

SPLIT-AILERON DRIVE BRAKES

FLIGHT INTERNATIONAL

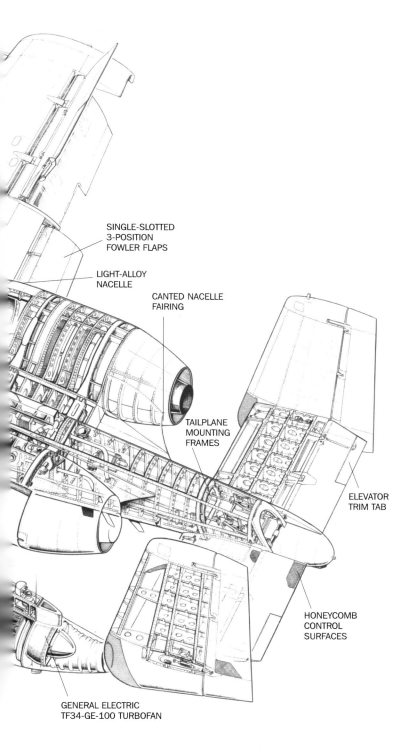

SINGLE-SLOTTED
3-POSITION
FOWLER FLAPS

LIGHT-ALLOY
NACELLE

CANTED NACELLE
FAIRING

TAILPLANE
MOUNTING
FRAMES

ELEVATOR
TRIM TAB

HONEYCOMB
CONTROL
SURFACES

GENERAL ELECTRIC
TF34-GE-100 TURBOFAN

and the head-up display and many electronic countermeasures were not yet installed, the A-10 clearly showed it was the superior aircraft. With congressional blessing, the A-10 moved into production. The first rolled off the assembly line in October 1975; the A-10 was officially ready for combat by the summer of 1978.

The Air Force envisioned A-10s as an aerial barrier that would stop the flow of Soviet tanks into Europe if the Cold War ever became hot. That battle never occurred, and the 713 production aircraft built by Fairchild remained untried in combat until the start of Operation Desert Storm in January 1991. By the end of the Gulf War, A-10s had flown 8100 sorties and launched 90 percent of the war's AGM-65s; later Air Force studies, however, questioned the effectiveness of A-10 strikes. Concerns have also been raised by officials in NATO countries concerning lingering health problems—principally a number of cancer deaths among peacekeeping soldiers in the Balkans who might have inhaled particles of depleted uranium, which forms the core of the Warthog's armor-piercing shells. This controversy is likely to outlive the A-10s themselves, many of which are now showing signs of fatigue in the form of tiny stress fractures in their airframes.

FIRE POWER

The Fairchild A-10 Warthog carries one of the world's most powerful guns, the GAU-8A 30mm Avenger. Larger than a compact car, it fires four different types of ammunition: armor-piercing incendiary, semi-armor-piercing high explosive, high-explosive incendiary, and target-practice rounds. The armor-piercing version contains a high-density depleted-uranium core that is especially effective versus tank armor. A typical "combat mix" consists of four of these rounds followed by one high-explosive incendiary round.

The Avenger's rounds, stored in a drum and loaded into the gun by a hydraulic-drive feeding system, are the size of wine bottles and weigh between 23 and 26 ounces. Casings from spent rounds are shuttled back to the drum.

To achieve its 3900 rounds-per-minute fire rate, the Avenger operates on the Gatling principle—a 26-hp electric motor rotates seven 30mm rifled barrels, whose bolts open and close as they follow a fixed cam.

Harriers similar to the one above, shown hovering over Camp Pendleton, California, were the Marine Corps' first strike aircraft to arrive in the Persian Gulf during Operation Desert Shield. From the sea, and also from land bases as near as 40 miles from the Kuwaiti border, the Marines flew 3380 sorties in Harrier aircraft during the ensuing war against Saddam Hussein's Iraqi forces.

AV-8B
Harrier II

• **McDonnell Douglas**

When the Marines say "Jump!" the AV-8B asks "How high?" These vertical-takeoff-and-landing attack jets can quickly rise to the occasion.

The advent of the jet engine in the late 1930s did more than lead to faster fighters and longer-range strategic bombers. It gave aeronautical engineers a powerplant around which to build a plane that had once existed only in their dreams—a fixed-wing aircraft that achieved the freedom of a bird by taking off and landing wherever the pilot pleased. Experimental vertical-takeoff-and-landing (VTOL) projects soon made headlines around the world. In 1954, Britain's Short Brothers placed five Rolls-Royce RB.108 engines on their SC.1. Four of them were mounted on gimbals beneath the fuselage and gently raised and lowered the small delta-winged aircraft, while a fifth in the tail provided thrust for level flight. Although the plane was shown off at the 1960 Farnborough Air Show and flew over the English Channel to participate in the Paris Air Show the following year, the multiengine arrangement proved overly complex, and a control failure caused the plane to crash in 1963, killing its pilot.

In the United States, Ryan Aircraft mounted a Rolls-Royce 10,000-pound-thrust engine in a slightly smaller delta-winged craft, the X-13 Vertijet. Unlike the SC.1, the Vertijet took off and landed on its tail, making its first ascent in May 1956. The following April it completed a full-cycle flight: a tail-sitting takeoff, the transition to horizontal flight and then the reverse for the tail-first landing. With the impossible now a reality, the X-13 ended its own life cycle several years later, as an exhibit in the U.S. Air Force Museum. French and German aircraft designers cooperated on the next VTOL, the Coleoptere, which resembled the nose of a jet fighter rising from an annular, keg-shaped wing. This new effort successfully flew in 1959. Unfortunately, during a subsequent attempt to make the transition to horizontal flight, it crashed.

The most successful of these projects, and the progenitor of the Harrier now flown by the U.S. Marine Corps, was the Hawker P.1127. Like the

American Harriers like the one above, taking off in 1985, have evolved into the day-attack Harrier II; a night-attack Harrier II; the Harrier II Plus, an AN/APG-65 radar-equipped, all-weather model that was the product of a multinational development program involving the United States, Spain and Italy; and the TAV-8B, a two-seat trainer version.

Short SC.1, it took off in a horizontal position. Instead of using separate jets for vertical flight, the P.1127 vented the blast of its relatively skimpy 11,000-pound-thrust engine earthward. Initial test flights sufficiently impressed NATO to encourage the British, U.S. and West German governments to invest in further development. A joint agreement between the Army, Navy and Air Force brought six of the British "jump jets" to the United States, where they were designated the XV-6A. In 1966 the Air Force began a series of tests on these new planes, including shipboard landings. The sea-launch capability impressed the Marine Corps, which then placed an order for the improved version of the P.1127 that the British Royal Air Force had designated the Harrier GR 1. The Marines designated these aircraft the AV-8A Harrier and placed them in service in the early 1970s.

McDonnell Douglas, which had become the American contractor for the Hawker-Siddley plane, now embarked upon an improvement program for the British import that, among other things, introduced a lighter, stronger composite wing. This work led to the AV-8B, which the Marine Corps subsequently adopted in the early 1980s.

The $23-million, single-seat aircraft has seven weapons stations—three on each wing and one

(continued)

VITALS	
Designation	AV-8B Harrier II
Wingspan	30 ft. 3 in.
Length	46 ft. 3 in.
Max. Weight	31,000 pounds (short takeoff)
	18,900 pounds (vert. takeoff)
Top Speed	1000 mph
Cruising Speed	630 mph
Range	722 miles with external fuel tanks (deck-launched intercept mission)
Ceiling	43,800 ft.

beneath the fuselage center line. The wing stations can accept external fuel pods or an assortment of air-to-ground ordnance, including AIM-9 Sidewinder missiles and AGM-65 Maverick missiles. The fuselage station was originally designed with twin 30mm Aden guns, later replaced by a six-barrel GAU-12 25mm gun system. The day-attack version is powered by a Rolls-Royce Pegasus F-402-series 20,280-pound-thrust turbofan. The night-attack and improved-radar models are equipped with an enhanced-thrust F-402-RR-408 engine.

The powerplants have not always operated flawlessly, however. In July 2000 the Marine Corps grounded over 100 of their Harrier strike aircraft due to a bearing problem with the Rolls-Royce F402-series turbofan; speedy repairs were completed less than a year later, and the entire fleet returned to operational status by May 2001.

THRUST VECTORING

The key to the Harrier's magic performance is its ability to divert both lift and propulsive thrust from one Rolls-Royce Pegasus turbofan engine through four swiveling exhaust nozzles. When the nozzles turn downward they can force the aircraft up during takeoff or slow its descent during landing. Once the Harrier is airborne it can fly horizontally when the nozzles swivel to their normal position.

Although the McDonnell Douglas AV-8B Harrier II represents the current state of the art in thrust-vectoring technology, mechanical nozzles are not the only way to direct exhaust flow.

NASA researchers have performed successful wind-tunnel testing using a technique called fluidic thrust vectoring. In this more recent technology, the path of a jet engine's exhaust stream can be influenced by the introduction of a secondary gas stream. Non-mechanical approaches offer the advantages of reducing both engine weight and the lag time for the vectoring system to react to a pilot's commands. Tests with NASA's experimental X-31 aircraft suggest that a fully developed thrust-vectoring system could one day lead to a revolutionary design innovation indeed—omitting an aircraft's vertical tail section altogether.

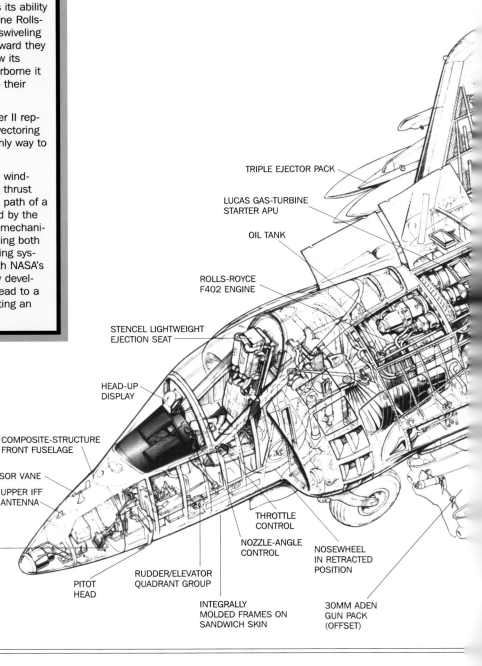

TRIPLE EJECTOR PACK

LUCAS GAS-TURBINE STARTER APU

OIL TANK

ROLLS-ROYCE F402 ENGINE

STENCEL LIGHTWEIGHT EJECTION SEAT

HEAD-UP DISPLAY

COMPOSITE-STRUCTURE FRONT FUSELAGE

YAW SENSOR VANE

UPPER IFF ANTENNA

PITCH REACTION-CONTROL NOZZLE

PITOT HEAD

RUDDER/ELEVATOR QUADRANT GROUP

THROTTLE CONTROL

NOZZLE-ANGLE CONTROL

NOSEWHEEL IN RETRACTED POSITION

INTEGRALLY MOLDED FRAMES ON SANDWICH SKIN

30MM ADEN GUN PACK (OFFSET)

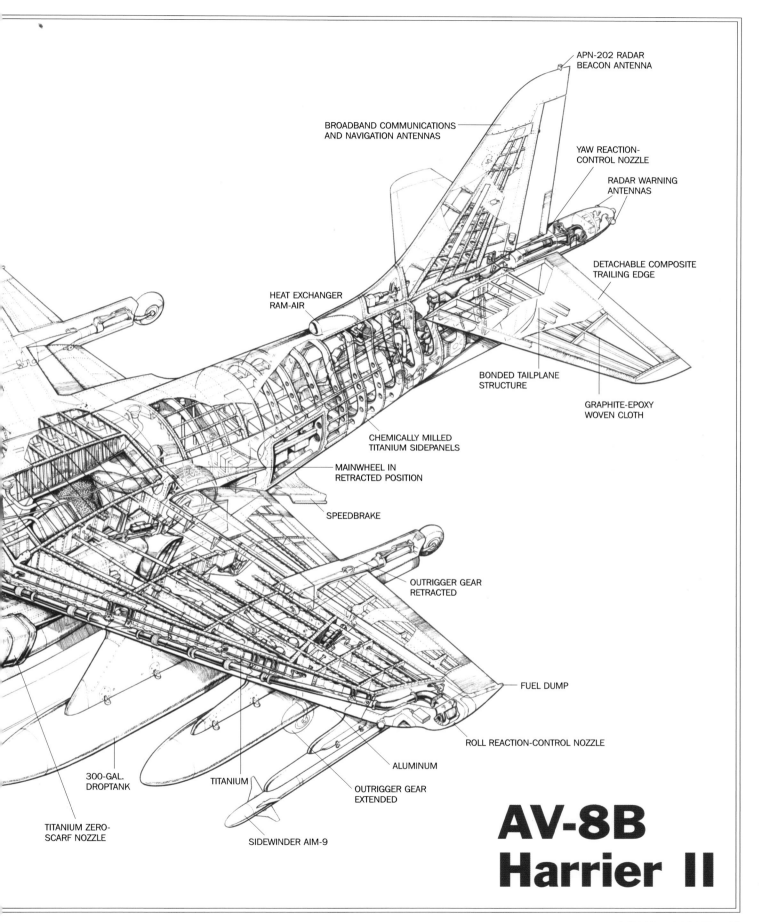

APN-202 RADAR
BEACON ANTENNA

BROADBAND COMMUNICATIONS
AND NAVIGATION ANTENNAS

YAW REACTION-
CONTROL NOZZLE

RADAR WARNING
ANTENNAS

DETACHABLE COMPOSITE
TRAILING EDGE

HEAT EXCHANGER
RAM-AIR

BONDED TAILPLANE
STRUCTURE

GRAPHITE-EPOXY
WOVEN CLOTH

CHEMICALLY MILLED
TITANIUM SIDEPANELS

MAINWHEEL IN
RETRACTED POSITION

SPEEDBRAKE

OUTRIGGER GEAR
RETRACTED

FUEL DUMP

ROLL REACTION-CONTROL NOZZLE

300-GAL.
DROPTANK

TITANIUM

ALUMINUM

OUTRIGGER GEAR
EXTENDED

TITANIUM ZERO-
SCARF NOZZLE

SIDEWINDER AIM-9

AV-8B
Harrier II

E-4B National Airborne Operations Center

CHAPTER 5

Reconnaissance and Electronic-Warfare Planes

The Lockheed U-2 (above) was the pioneer of high-altitude strategic reconnaissance, with a design that allowed for an operational ceiling far exceeding that of any 1950s-era aircraft. Its initial mission, Operation Overflight—conducting reconnaissance flights that violated Soviet airspace—ended in embarrassment when U-2 pilot Francis Gary Powers was shot down over Sverdlovsk in May 1960.

Spyplanes & Electronics

As the eyes, ears and coordinators of the skies, these aircraft often fly in the murky territory between war and peace. The fruits of their intelligence-gathering missions are vital to national security.

The first U.S. military planes were not bombers, fighters or attack aircraft but replacements for balloon-powered observation platforms. It was with such intelligence-gathering in mind that the U.S. Army assigned its first Wright Flyer to the Signals Corps, the same unit that conducted aerial reconnaissance missions from hydrogen-filled balloons during the Civil War. The obvious advantage of a heavier-than-air flying machine over a balloon is its power over the unpredictable whims of the wind. A less obvious and almost counter-intuitive advantage is an airplane's ceiling. Military balloons must be tethered lest they land in enemy territory,

but high-flying aircraft can spot approaching troops hours before they reach the battle line; swooping low, planes can provide an even more valuable service by identifying an opposing force's unit designation. This information was (and still is) critical to commanders in the field who could then check existing intelligence on the unit in question and deploy their own forces accordingly.

As sophisticated as today's observation, reconnaissance and electronic-warfare aircraft have become, the underlying missions of their crews remain the same as those of the brave souls who have infiltrated enemy territory ever since the dawn of com-

The Navy's P-3 Orion was a high-performance antisub aircraft with weather-reconnaissance and electronic-reconnaissance variants. In addition to the P-3's extensive standard-electronics package in the fuselage, these spy versions carried specialized radar housed in three radomes around the aircraft's body.

NASA's SR-71B, a nonmilitary pilot-training model based at Dryden Flight Research Center, knifed over the Sierra Nevada mountains after a refueling run.

The Curtiss O-52 Owl (above) was the last of the armed O-designation aircraft acquired in large numbers by the U.S. Army Air Corps. The two-seater, delivered in the early 1940s, was deemed too slow and light to defend itself (despite two .30-cal. machine guns) and too heavy—it needed a take-off run of 1000 ft.—for small-field operations required to support ground troops.

bat: They are essentially scouts. Now, however, cameras and electronic devices enable them to interpret the world beyond the limitations of the naked eye. To understand how reconnaissance and electronic-warfare aircraft see the unseen, we need to recall some high-school physics and examine the veritable sea of electromagnetic energy.

Electromagnetic energy contributes to everything from bonding atoms, to making molecules, to creating heat, to perking the morning coffee. At so-called "optical frequencies," this energy nudges the molecules in the rods and cones of the retina of the human eye, setting into motion a chain of biochemical activity our brains interpret as sight.

Beyond the visible spectrum, where energy waves oscillate just below the frequencies we perceive as the color red, is the infrared region. Electronic sensors on reconnaissance aircraft "tuned" to this portion of the electromagnetic spectrum can detect the faint heat emitted by warm bodies

and the hot exhaust left behind by jet engines. The next step down on the spectrum is occupied by microwaves, which—in addition to popping corn in 3-5 minutes—provide frequencies used by most radar systems. Lower still are frequency ranges used for communications. These energy waves are least inhibited by buildings and structures—and the most energetic among them tend to move unimpeded through the magnetic field that enrobes the Earth. Measured from thousands, to hundreds of millions of cycles per second, or hertz, these radio waves are useful for short-range, line-of-sight military communications. Extremely low-frequency waves (ELF), less than 1000 hertz, also have military value as the only frequencies capable of penetrating the depths of the sea and transmitting emergency orders to ballistic-missile-carrying submarines.

The physics of the electromagnetic spectrum have led to three specific types of aircraft. Generally, military aircraft with the designation O are observation planes that monitor the visible light regions. Most are assigned to tactical units within the Army and fly missions that are little changed from the days when scouts went aloft in the wicker baskets of hydrogen balloons.

Planes designated R are reconnaissance aircraft, which photograph enemy installations with high-resolution cameras; they also bathe the Earth in the invisible light of radar then use the returned signals to create detailed 3D maps of the terrain below. One of their most important missions is eavesdropping on tactical communications and radar transmitters. During the Cold War, American reconnaissance aircraft routinely probed the fringes of Soviet airspace with the specific intent of making defenders turn on their short-range radar. In much the same way that nuances in the human voice reflect something about the person speaking, radar tells the trained observer a considerable amount about a potential adversary's capabilities. Analyzing signals from Russian-built radar stations has made it possible for the United States and its allies to develop radar-jamming and other countermeasure systems that have now become as intrinsic to a modern combat aircraft as the radio.

Military aircraft designated E for electronics use computers to sort through the entire electromagnetic spectrum to form a 3D image of the visible and invisible sky. This information allows the military to keep tabs on potential enemies and their movements. In combat, planes with this capability turn the sky into a kind of deadly computerized video game, in which each aircraft within sensor range is identified and its position precisely tracked.

In the pages ahead are four of the most important reconnaissance and electronic-warfare aircraft: the Lockheed U-2, which, among other surveillance coups, identified the presence of Soviet missiles in Cuba in 1962; the Lockheed SR-71, the fastest and highest-flying spyplane ever built; the Boeing E-3 AWACS, which tracks potentially hostile aircraft and coordinates the strikes against them; and finally, the Boeing E-4B, the "doomsday" airborne command center designed to survive a nuclear war.

The Grumman OV-1 Mohawk (above) was a versatile, durable tactical-reconnaissance aircraft that served the U.S. Army from the late 1950s through Operation Desert Storm. Mohawks were modified for photography, infrared imaging, electronic surveillance and intelligence gathering; some were even converted to gunships. The Army retired the Mohawk from service in 1996.

When the McDonnell F-4 Phantom II traded in its heat-seeking missiles for cameras, the result was the RF-4C, a supersonic tactical-reconnaissance jet that proved valuable during Vietnam. During the Gulf War, RF-4Cs flew more missions than any other F-4 aircraft.

Aside from flights over the Soviet Union, the U-2 (above) has also flown missions over China, Cuba, Southeast Asia, the Middle East and other areas of interest to the U.S. intelligence community. A variant that was structurally identical to the U-2R, the TR-1, was charged with stand-off tactical reconnaissance missions. In the early 1990s, however, these planes were re-designated as U-2Rs.

U-2
Dragon Lady

• Lockheed

The fragile, gliderlike aircraft captured images that tripped a political chain reaction and pushed the world to the brink of nuclear war.

The lowering of the Iron Curtain over Eastern Europe forced the West to formulate new intelligence-gathering policies. In the early 1950s the U.S. Air Force began developing plans for a stratospheric one-seat reconnaissance aircraft—essentially an ultra-high-resolution camera with a jet engine and a pair of wings. With a sky-high ceiling of over 65,000 ft., the new spyplane was expected to elude Soviet radar and interceptors. After catching wind of the proposal, Lockheed submitted an unsolicited design by the legendary Clarence "Kelly" Johnson

for an aircraft called the CL-282, which the Air Force initially rejected. But the design had its supporters, and Lockheed was given the green light after President Eisenhower and the Central Intelligence Agency signed on. It was the intelligence agency, however, that was assigned primary responsibility for the new joint CIA-USAF overflight reconnaissance program—which it code-named Aquatone. The first aircraft, given the Air Force designation U-2, for Utility—meant to conceal its true mission—made its maiden flight on August 4,

VITALS	
Designation	U-2S Dragon Lady
Wingspan	103 ft.
Length	63 ft.
Max. Weight	41,000 pounds
Top Speed	Approximately 500 mph
Cruising Speed	460 mph
Range	4600 miles
Ceiling	Believed to be 90,000 ft.

1955. U-2 aircraft became operational in the summer of 1956.

The essence of simplicity, the U-2 was designed with straight, narrow wings and bicycle-type landing gear to save weight. Additionally, the tail assembly was attached to the main body with just three bolts. The pilot wore (and still wears) a heated, fully pressurized suit to prevent his body fluids from boiling off and his eyeballs from freezing in the spacelike environment at flight altitudes.

Although highly secret, the spyplane's existence became public in dramatic fashion in 1960 when U-2 pilot Francis Gary Powers was shot down over the Soviet Union and captured; U.S.S.R. radar and missile defenses had been grossly underestimated. Powers's well-publicized trial revealed that U.S. spyplanes had been secretly violating Soviet airspace to photograph military installations. Two years later, in perhaps the defining moment of the Cold War, the U-2 again took center stage: One of its flights over Cuba produced photos of Soviet-built nuclear-missile sites just 90 miles from the U.S. coast—a revelation that precipitated the U.S. naval blockade. Both episodes eventually ended peacefully: Powers was exchanged for a Soviet spy after spending nearly two years in a Russian prison, and the Cuban Missile Crisis was defused when Soviet premier Nikita Khrushchev backed down.

Although the U-2 program, called Project Dragon Lady by the Air Force, slipped from the headlines, the success of its opera-

tions encouraged Lockheed to develop several different versions. The U-2R, first flown in 1967, had a larger wingspan, a heavier payload capacity and a reputed ceiling of 80,000 ft. No longer secret, the aircraft was also made available in 1981 to NASA, which uses it for Earth-resources research under the designation ER-2. The current generation of U-2S aircraft, powered by a General Electric F-118-101 19,000-pound-thrust turbofan, can be quickly reconfigured with modular cameras and sensors for different missions—mapping studies, atmospheric sampling and 3D imaging.

Camera photography, however, remains the forte of the U-2. Perhaps its two most important tools are the HR-329 "H-cam," a high-resolution gyroscope-stabilized framer with a 66-in. focal length; and IRIS, the Intelligence Reconnaissance Imagery System III, which provides less resolution but can photograph a broad zone below the aircraft that is 32 nautical miles wide.

As a curious postscript, the U-2 also contributed to one of the most enduring myths of recent memory: UFO sightings. Air Force analysts working on Project Blue Book compared the sightings with flight logs of the U-2 and SR-71 (another high-flying U.S. spyplane). In 1998 the CIA disclosed long-secret findings that more than half of the UFO sightings of the late 1950s and most of the 1960s could be attributed to flights of these secret military aircraft.

The original U-2 (above) gave birth to a long-lived line of bigger and better successors. Current U-2s sport a stronger engine, keener sensors and redesigned cockpit displays. The Air Force reportedly plans to keep the fleet operational until 2020.

A closeup view of the SR-71's smooth, rounded edges (above) conjures visions of a giant sting ray with two Pratt & Whitney engines fused to its body. Although the development of the Blackbird's distinctive airframe led to several innovations in radar-absorbing technology, the SR-71 was hardly a stealth aircraft. Infrared sensors could easily pick up heat from its powerful engines.

SR-71
Blackbird

• Lockheed

No jet-powered aircraft has flown higher or faster than this legendary, sleek spyplane. Much of its 30-year history is still cloaked in secrecy.

In 1957, three years before a Soviet missile downed U-2 pilot Francis Gary Powers, the Department of Defense realized that if the United States wanted to continue aerial reconnaissance over Russia it would need a faster, higher-flying aircraft. The government subsequently asked Lockheed, developer of the U-2, and General Dynamics, one of Lockheed's chief competitors, to present designs for a new spyplane that could fly nearly twice as high and four times faster than the

U-2. In August 1959, a Lockheed design was selected, and work began on a spyplane that would at various times be known as the A-11, A-12, B-71, RS-71, SR-71, SR-71A, YF-12A and Blackbird. More than 40 years later they remain the world's fastest and highest-flying jet-powered aircraft.

The first versions, the A-11 and a variant with a smaller radar cross-section, the A-12, were ordered for the CIA as part of a project code-named Oxcart. A silvery A-12 made its first flight on April 26,

VITALS

Designation	SR-71A Blackbird
Wingspan	55 ft. 7 in.
Length	107 ft. 5 in.
Max. Weight	140,000 pounds
Top Speed	Over 2000 mph (mach 3+)
Cruising Speed	335 mph
Range	Over 2900 miles
Ceiling	Officially above 85,000 ft. Believed to be above 100,000 ft.

1962. Seeing the plane's potential, the U.S. Air Force ordered a modified A-12, a reconnaissance aircraft eventually called the SR-71 Blackbird, which flew for the first time on December 22, 1964.

The long, delta-wing planes are still a marvel of aerospace engineering. Flying three times faster than the speed of sound confronts engineers with a host of design challenges. At Mach 3, friction created by the rapid passage of molecules heats the airframe to temperatures that damage aviation-grade aluminum. Thus, designs for the A-12 and the SR-71 called for titanium and titanium alloy. For additional heat protection, the windscreen was fashioned from fused quartz; a special black, heat-dissipating paint job earned the spyplane the nickname Blackbird. Another temperature-related oddity was the fuel tanks. Designed to allow for in-flight expansion, they often leaked when the SR-71 sat on the runway.

To attain the high speeds at which the Air Force was sure the Blackbird would be safe from any anti-aircraft missile, the plane was equipped with a pair of Pratt & Whitney J-58 axial-flow turbojets. With afterburners, each produced 32,500 pounds of thrust. During a typical two-hour flight, they burned 20 tons of a specially formulated JP-7 fuel.

The A-12 proved so successful at high-altitude photo reconnais-

sance that the Air Force considered making it the basis for many new variants: not only reconnaissance planes, but also fighters, bombers and launch vehicles that would send drone spyplanes over high-risk targets. The technical aspects of mastering this new, faster realm of flight was so difficult that the Air Force offered NASA two of its YF-12A fighter prototypes for flight tests in exchange for the space agency's expertise.

Despite ambitious plans for several iterations of SR-71-like aircraft, the Air Force only successfully operated the reconnaissance version. The SR-71A had a two-man crew outfitted in space suits: The pilot sat in the forward cockpit, while a systems operator occupied a rear station and monitored sensors. During high-speed, high-altitude missions, the SR-71 is believed to have routinely flown above 100,000 ft. Chief among the myths generated by the Blackbird's existence is the persistent belief

(continued)

Two crewmen, decked out in space suits (above), posed with their SR-71 on the tarmac. Candidates to fly the elegantly designed spyplane—which pilots called the "Sled"—underwent a one-week interview process at Beale AFB.

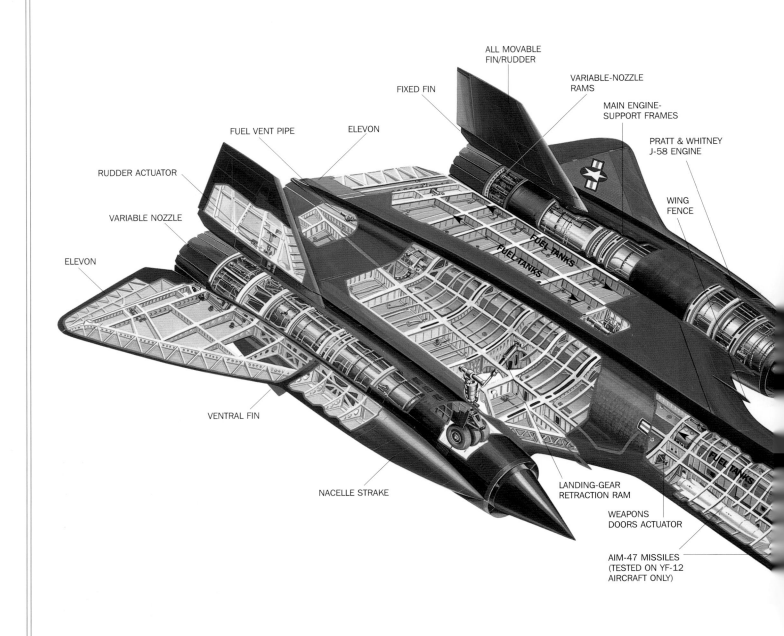

ALL MOVABLE
FIN/RUDDER

VARIABLE-NOZZLE
RAMS

FIXED FIN

MAIN ENGINE-
SUPPORT FRAMES

FUEL VENT PIPE

ELEVON

PRATT & WHITNEY
J-58 ENGINE

RUDDER ACTUATOR

WING
FENCE

VARIABLE NOZZLE

FUEL TANKS

FUEL TANKS

ELEVON

VENTRAL FIN

FUEL TANKS

LANDING-GEAR
RETRACTION RAM

NACELLE STRAKE

WEAPONS
DOORS ACTUATOR

AIM-47 MISSILES
(TESTED ON YF-12
AIRCRAFT ONLY)

SR-71A Blackbird

that it was a stealthy aircraft. Nothing could be further from the truth. With its exhaust serving as an infrared calling card, the Blackbird could be detected hundreds of miles away.

The Air Force's shift in focus to satellites and truly stealthy craft led to the deactivation of its last SR-71 group in 1990. The Blackbird was briefly recalled from retirement in the mid-1990s, but operational costs led to a second cancellation before the end of the decade. Over the course of these remarkable planes' collective history, the CIA and the Air Force together owned some 51 aircraft; 19 were lost in various mishaps. The last organization to fly the SR-71 was NASA, which maintains two civilianized Blackbirds in "flyable storage."

Although some details of the CIA Oxcart flights have come to light in the past decade—nearly 30 missions were flown over Southeast Asia and China by A-12 pilots from Kadena Air Base in Japan—less has been revealed about SR-71 missions. It is impossible, therefore, to assess whether these unique aircraft lived up to their true intelligence-gathering potential.

CONE ACTUATOR

INTAKE DIFFUSER CONE

FUEL PUMPS

REFUELING PROBE RECEPTACLE

PORT AVIONICS BAY

SYSTEMS-OPERATOR EJECTION SEAT

PILOT EJECTION SEAT

INFRARED SENSOR

AN/ASG-18 RADAR

RADAR ANTENNA

AIR-CONDITIONING PLANT

STARBOARD OXYGEN TANKS

NOSEWHEEL

PITOT HEAD

AIRCRAFT DESIGNATION

The SR-71 is probably the only warplane ever designated by "mistake." In 1964, President Johnson announced the existence of the SR-71 (Strategic Reconnaissance), changing the RS-71 (Reconnaissance Strike) designation for which the aircraft was slated. Rather than correct the commander in chief, the Air Force retained the "new" name.

Designations tell a good deal about an aircraft. The starting point for the current unified Army, Navy, Air Force scheme is the hyphen. The first letter to the left describes the mission. Attack aircraft are designated with an A, bombers B, cargo C, electronics E, fighters F, observation O, reconnaissance R, and trainer T.

Additionally, the letter S stands for antisubmarine, not surveillance. H indicates a helicopter. V refers to other types of vertical or short-takeoff-and-landing aircraft such as the V-22 tilt-rotor. A second letter provides detail or describes a secondary mission. OH indicates an observation helicopter, UH a utility helicopter, AH an attack helicopter. The K in KC-135 stands for kerosene, indicating this plane is a tanker. An RC-135 is the same basic C-135 cargo plane with reconnaissance gear. Research aircraft are X-planes, as in the X-15 rocket plane. The letter Y indicates than an aircraft is undergoing service tests in anticipation of being put into production.

The number to the right of the hyphen indicates a specific aircraft. When the Department of Defense put its new designation plan into effect in 1962, it reset the numbering system to one. The letter A follows the first plane put into service, the letter B indicates an upgraded version and so on, through the alphabet.

In addition to the more than 30 active E-3s in the U.S. fleet, the Boeing 707-based AWACS aircraft (above) serves several air forces around the world, including those of France, the United Kingdom, Saudi Arabia and the North Atlantic Treaty Organization (NATO).

E-3
Sentry

• **Boeing**

Flying far from the battle space, E-3 Airborne Warning and Control System aircraft call the shots for a virtual chessboard of warplanes.

Looking at the large, awkward dome sprouting from the top of its fuselage, one has trouble imagining that the Boeing E-3 Airborne Warning and Control System (AWACS) can fly at all. That instantly recognizable mushroom-like structure, however, makes the E-3 arguably one of the most important aircraft in the U.S. Air Force arsenal, for it contains the antennas that enable the Sentry to search for other aircraft and provides the

plane's computers with the necessary information to identify the contacts.

Designed around a militarized version of the Boeing 707-320B commercial airliner and powered by four Pratt & Whitney TF33 21,000-pound-thrust turbofans, the E-3 Sentry is an extremely mobile and eminently survivable observation platform that can quickly move from one tactically important location to another. Via its powerful "look-down" radar, the E-3 can probe through ground and sea interference and pick out military units in the air and at sea. Once a target is spotted, AWACS computers tag it and follow its progress, even if the contact dips to low altitudes. A color-coded "friend-or foe" identification system clearly defines the battle space—a 360-degree view of a virtual horizon that can extend as far as 200 miles—for the E-3's 13 to 19 mission specialists, who operate the tracking systems and direct Air Force fighters to intercept hostile bogeys. Additionally, the Sentry has a flight crew of four.

The U.S. Air Force took delivery of the first of its 34 AWACS aircraft in March 1977, and the last was delivered in June 1984. Since then they have gone back to the shop for a series of upgrades to their electronic systems, including the recent addition of Global Positioning Satellite systems to pinpoint an E-3's location anywhere in the world.

The most significant upgrade is a passive surveillance capability that enables E-3 aircraft to pick-up, identify and monitor electronic transmissions from land-, air- or sea-based sources. Mission operators can now identify specific types of enemy radar and the weapons associated with them without emitting the signals that might disclose a Sentry's location.

AWACS aircraft proved their value during Desert Shield and Desert Storm, providing surveillance during the former and monitoring some 120,000

The rotodome of the E-3 Sentry (above) sits 11 ft. above the fuselage. The Radar System Improvement Program, a mutinational effort, enhances current 707 AWACS with a more sensitive Doppler radar (tuned for stealthier targets) better electronic countermeasures, upgraded computers and redesigned radar consoles.

coalition-aircraft sorties during the latter. After the air war broke out, over 400 E-3 missions were flown, for a total of 5000 hours in the air. During this time, the controllers who staffed AWACS consoles directed air strikes, guided coalition fighters toward Iraqi airplanes, coordinated air-to-air refueling flights and protected aircraft involved in intelligence-gathering and ground surveillance. Sentry aircrews had a hand in the destruction of nearly all of the 41 Iraqi planes shot down during the conflict.

Production of the Boeing 707 airliner ended in May 1991, which halted the propagation of the E-3 Sentry as well. The next generation of early-warning aircraft were four Boeing 767-based AWACS—with 50 percent more floor space and nearly twice the volume of the 707—made operational in Japan's Air Force in May 2000. Boeing is currently under contract with the government of Australia to build a new 737-700-based Airborne Early Warning and Control (AEWC) platform, which will sport up-to-date avionics and replace the familiar AWACS dome with a low-drag "top hat" structure.

Despite these recent iterations of the air-based long-range observation platform, the U.S. Air Force intends to keep its current AWACS fleet flying as long as possible. Air Combat Command's Extend Sentry program should keep the E-3 in fighting trim through the year 2025.

VITALS	
Designation	E-3B Sentry
Wingspan	145 ft. 9 in.
Length	144 ft. 10 in.
Rotodome	30 ft. diameter, 6 ft. thick
Max. Weight	335,000 pounds
Top Speed	530 mph
Cruising Speed	360 mph
Range	1000 miles (6 hours on station)
Ceiling	35,000 ft.

The Boeing E-4B National Airborne Operations Center (above) was hardened to survive the effects of an electromagnetic pulse—the tidal wave of energy radiated by a nuclear explosion. Detonating only a few nuclear bombs at an optimum altitude above North America could potentially short-circuit every unprotected electronic device from coast to coast and render civilian communications useless.

E-4

National Airborne Operations Center

• Boeing

Designed to remain operational in all scenarios—even a nuclear war—the E-4 keeps a constant vigil for the National Command Authority.

In the event of a national emergency, the Boeing E-4B National Airborne Operations Center (NAOC) is poised to spring into action as a flying command post for the president, the secretary of defense and/or their successors—collectively known as the National Command Authority.

Although the U.S. Air Force inventory contains only four such "Doomsday" planes—ominously named, for even nuclear warfare can be waged from inside their airframes—the aircraft themselves are well known to the flying public: The E-4B NAOC is a militarized and in-flight-

VITALS	
Designation	E-4B National Airborne Operations Center
Wingspan	195 ft. 8 in.
Length	231 ft. 4 in.
Max. Weight	800,000 pounds
Top Speed	602 mph
Cruising Speed	560 mph
Endurance	12 hours unrefueled
Ceiling	Over 30,000 ft.

The National Command Authority and senior officials travel in relative comfort—a main cabin appointed in fire-resistant Nomex and no-pile carpeting, a small in-flight working office, a briefing room and a rest area. The crew shares a nearby dorm room. Accommodations farther back in the cabin are more functional and can house a small army for battle-staff operations: The E-4B supports up to 114 people all told.

The only part of the plane that can be described as first class is the communications equipment. Doomsday-plane radios can operate across the electromagnetic spectrum, from frequencies just above direct current to those in the range of light. A 5-mile-long low-frequency antenna deploys from the plane's tail, and satellite dishes enclosed behind a fairing added to the top of the fuselage connect the plane with the Milstar military communications network and civilian telecommunication satellites. Together, they enable the president to speak with any commander in any service, dial any

(continued)

refuelable version of the world's first jumbo jet, the Boeing 747-200.

The Doomsday fleet operates from Offutt AFB, Nebraska, on what is formally known as the Nightwatch mission. When the president travels abroad, the E-4B follows and is frequently mistaken for Air Force 1, which technically speaking is any plane in which the president is sitting, although usually a Boeing 747 with similar livery. At least one Doomsday plane is always on alert status at one of several bases throughout the world.

In late 1974 the Air Force began accepting its first widebody command posts, designated the E-4A. The first B version was delivered in January 1980, and the three existing A models were subsequently upgraded so that by 1985 the fleet consisted of four E-4B aircraft.

Although the E-4B looks like a garden-variety Boeing 747-200 and flies on one of its power-plant configurations—four General Electric CF6-50E2 turbofans of 52,500 pounds-thrust apiece—the Doomsday plane has features unlike any other aircraft, American or otherwise. Differences begin with the airframe, which is chock full of heat, noise and electromagnetic-field-pulse shielding. As with many commercial aircraft, there is a difference between accommodations in the front and the back of the plane.

A flight engineer (above) with the 1st Airborne Command and Control Squadron, based at Offutt Air Force Base, Nebraska, concentrated his efforts on a wall-sized instrument panel while completing a pre-flight check aboard an E-4B. The Joint Chiefs of Staff control E-4B operations and provide much of its personnel.

telephone number on the planet and, if necessary, break into any commercial radio or television broadcast. Not surprisingly, these capabilities require a considerable amount of energy to power the communications gear and run the air conditioning system that cools it. The Air Force calculates that the E-4B uses about as much power as a town of 15,000 people.

In August 1994 the Nightwatch mission was expanded. With the permission of the chairman of the Joint Chiefs of Staff, the E-4B can act as a command and control center for the Federal Emergency Management Agency until FEMA's own natural disaster response team becomes operational.

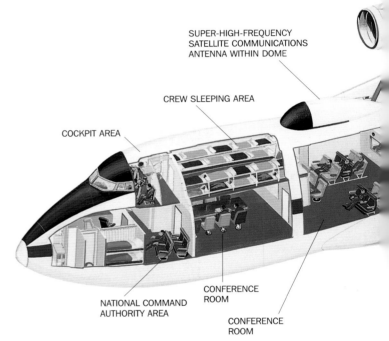

SUPER-HIGH-FREQUENCY
SATELLITE COMMUNICATIONS
ANTENNA WITHIN DOME

CREW SLEEPING AREA

COCKPIT AREA

NATIONAL COMMAND
AUTHORITY AREA

CONFERENCE
ROOM

CONFERENCE
ROOM

IN PM'S WORDS

Doomsday's Inner Sanctum

"Now we'll take you on a tour of the E-4B, starting with the stateroom suite. These deluxe facilities are furnished with a desk, conference area, double-deck bunks, private toilet facilities and other touches to accommodate the National Command Authority—the president, a member of the Joint Chiefs or a duly designated representative.

"Let's walk fore to aft through the four other major compartments that make up the main deck space.

"First is the high-level conference room, dominated by a 9-person table.... The next room back—the largest on the airplane—is the battle-staff compartment, which provides about 30 desks for intelligence, logistics and operations planners, various controllers for force status, emergency actions, operations and communications, plus weather, reconnaissance and other officers. Airborne Launch Control System officers would also sit here.

"Next aft is the communications area, which divides voice and data links longitudinally. A staff of 15 ... operates and monitors all communications facilities. A stairway from this compartment leads down to the aft lower-lobe equipment areas, which include an electronics maintenance shop and a control station for the hydraulic winch that reels and stores the trailing-wire VLF antenna."

—Kenneth J. Stein
POPULAR MECHANICS, May 1994

E-4B NAOC

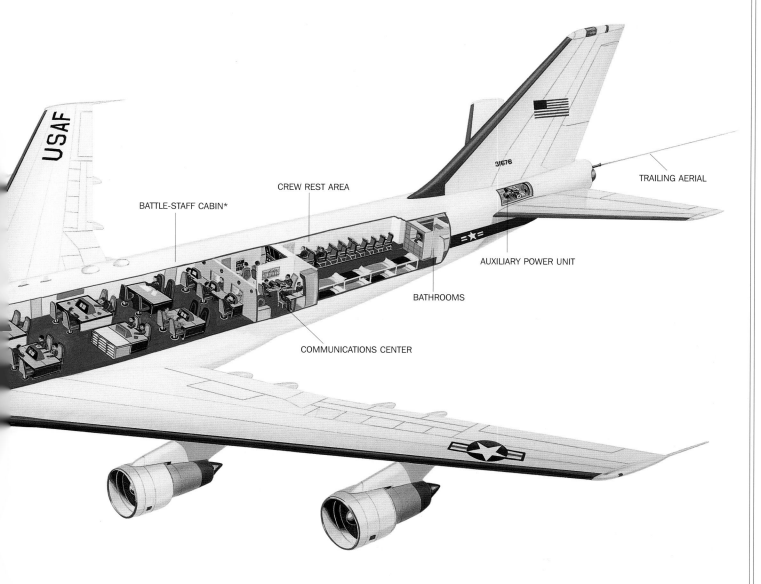

BATTLE-STAFF CABIN*

CREW REST AREA

TRAILING AERIAL

AUXILIARY POWER UNIT

BATHROOMS

COMMUNICATIONS CENTER

USAF

31676

* TYPICAL BATTLE-STAFF COMPLEMENT:

5 RADIO-MAINTENANCE ENGINEERS
5 RECORD COMMUNICATIONS OPERATORS
4 LOGISTICS PLANNERS
4 INTELLIGENCE PLANNERS
3 RADIO OPERATORS
3 FORCE STATUS CONTROLLERS
2 AIRBORNE-LAUNCH-SYSTEM OFFICERS
2 SWITCHBOARD OPERATORS
1 RECONNAISSANCE PLANNER
1 DAMAGE ASSESSMENT OFFICER
1 WEATHER OFFICER
1 COMMUNICATIONS CONTROLLER
1 EMERGENCY-ACTIONS NCO
1 CHIEF, BATTLE STAFF

Lockheed C-130 Hercules

Two McDonnell Douglas C-17s (above) scattered huge pallets of cargo like trails of bread crumbs in the waiting sky. The massive aircraft can accommodate over a hundred paratroopers or more than 170,000 pounds of freight. Eight of these powerful cargo planes flew over 9200 miles and dropped troops and equipment during a 19-hour-plus mission—a world record for airdrops—in 1998.

Fighters, Freight and Fuel

The best-trained fighting force in the world would go nowhere without a reliable ride. Ferrying combatants and replenishing the planes that support them is a crucial brushstroke in the art of war.

Despite the low speed, short range and limited carrying capacity of World War I aircraft, it was evident to forward-looking military planners that airplanes would one day fulfill the important mission of transporting fighting men and weapons to battle zones. Aircraft endurance demonstrations performed in the 1920s suggested an additional tactical possibility for airplanes—aerial refueling. With its aircraft's fuel tanks replenished in flight, the United States could extend its global reach—previously achieved at the beginning of the 20th century with naval fleets alone—through the strength of air power.

By a twist of fate, transport aircraft revealed their potential at precisely the wrong moment in history, as America began its long slide into the Great Depression. Desirable though specialized military transports were, pursuit aircraft and bombers were given budgetary priority; it was decided that Army transports would have to come "off the shelf" as civilian aircraft adapted for military missions. Although it could not be foreseen at the time, this collision of emerging need with limited funds would actually work to the benefit of both the military and the commercial aviation industries.

It takes four Pratt & Whitney engines with a combined thrust of 122,000 pounds to heft the bulbous C-17 Globemaster III to its operational ceiling of 45,000 ft.

Two naval jets took a long drink from a Lockheed C-130 in 1957 (above). The Navy often employs a different refueling system than the Air Force—from its wing the tanker lets out a basketlike drogue and hose, into which the "customer" plane flies its refueling probe. Two aircraft can refuel at the same time. The versatile C-130 has been adapted for attack, electronics-jamming and many other missions.

One of the first military aircraft to carry the C designation (for cargo) was the Atlantic-Fokker C-2, an improved version of the distinctive Fokker F-VIIA-3M, a trimotor passenger plane from the mid-1920s. This trend continued with the Douglas C-47 Skytrain—praised by then Supreme Allied Commander Dwight D. Eisenhower as one of the most important weapons of World War II—which was simply a toughened version of the DC-3, the plane that helped to create the modern commercial aviation industry. This military-civilian relationship continues today. The McDonnell Douglas KC-10 tanker (kerosene cargo), which the U.S. Air Force intends to keep flying until the middle of the 21st century, is a converted DC-10 widebody jet. There are, of course, specialized military transports built from the ground up that handle special conditions, such as short and primitive runways. But in large measure, today's military cargo planes mirror those available for civilian transport.

The symbiotic relationship between defense and commercial transport has proven to be healthy for both military and civil aviation. In the case of the KC-10, for example, the airline industry's widespread use of the DC-10 on international routes has assured that spare parts and maintenance expertise are globally available. The military additionally benefits by employing commercial pilots—who maintain their KC-10 flying skills by commanding DC-10 airliners—as part of its reserve force. For the airline industry, Air Force-trained aviators remain a ready and willing pool of first officers.

In terms of airlifts, the military distinguishes among three variations. Strategic-airlift commands use massive cargo planes to move weapons and fast-response forces from the continental United States to theaters of war around the world. Separate, smaller airlift operations are organized within this overall battle zone—around the Persian Gulf during Operations Desert Shield and Desert Storm, for example. The third, most narrowly focused type of airlift is conducted with what the military calls "organic" aircraft, typically

The Fairchild C-119 Flying Boxcar served America in Korea and Vietnam. In 1960 a C-119 snatched the re-entering Discoverer XIV satellite by its parachute for a precision mid-air recovery.

The colossal Lockheed C-5 Galaxy has a staggering 222-ft. wingspan and can carry up to 329 personnel. With its gaping forward cargo door open, it can gobble up anything the Army has to transport—tanks, helicopters or a 74-ton mobile bridge.

The Lockheed C-141 Starlifter (above) was the Air Force's first all-jet-powered cargo aircraft. With 30 different configurations, it has been a workhorse for the U.S. military since 1965, logging nearly 9 million air hours. The Starlifter can carry over 200 ground troops or nearly 170 paratroopers. With a maximum payload of over 94,000 pounds, its range is an impressive 2878 miles.

helicopters that share hostile airspace with flying bullets. Most organic aircraft units operate under Army aviation and naval aviation programs.

A critical, but often misunderstood, aspect of the airlift mission is the simple act of putting warriors and weapons on the ground. Even in wartime, men and matériel usually arrive as they do in peacetime: The aircraft lands, passengers deplane and cargo is unloaded—what the Air Force calls "airland" delivery. The second method, aerial delivery, is the in-flight deployment of personnel and pallets of supplies from the doors of low-flying aircraft. Early aerial delivery, in addition to influencing the development of parachute airdrops and airborne fighting units, led to a specialized type of aircraft unique to World War II, the Waco CG-2A Hadrian combat glider. Towed behind a motorized transport, typically a C-47-class aircraft, the one-use glider was released over the landing zone and simply left behind after it touched down and its contents were unloaded.

Looking ahead, the most dramatic change for airlift operations is likely to come with the introduction of fully automated aircraft. The move from manned to unmanned aerial vehicles is being driven by two developments: the advent of the Global Positioning Satellite (GPS) system, which provides a reliable means of guiding unmanned craft to landing sites; and on-board artificial intelligence systems, which can identify enemy threats and instruct the aircraft to take the appropriate evasive actions. A more subtle change in airlift policy involves the timing of the delivery of weapons and warriors. Increasingly, weapons, including advanced aircraft, have been pre-positioned near trouble spots, and reserve units have been called upon to take an earlier role in combat. It is not inconceivable that in some future war, weekend-warrior pilots will earn "frequent flyer" miles as they take commercial airlines to cities on the outskirts of war zones, and replacement parts for their aircraft will arrive via overnight shipping.

Omnipresent over every World War II theater, the Douglas C-47 Skytrain (above) buzzed the pyramids at Giza in the early 1940s. By mid-1945 nearly 10,000 C-47s had been built for the U.S. Army Air Forces. It remains one of history's most celebrated aircraft.

C-47
Skytrain

• Douglas

The "Gooney Bird" was the most faithful aerial pack horse of World War II. Some 60 years later the DC-3, its parent, still graces the skies.

Like millions of young Americans, the Douglas DC-3 commercial airliner was drafted to serve in World War II. Its tour of duty began in 1940 when the Army ordered 250 of the low-wing twin-engine planes as paratrooper transports. Designated the C-53 Skytrooper, the plane became the first member of the DC-3 family to go to war. The most familiar militarized version of the DC-3 was the C-47 cargo plane. A versatile, dependable aircraft that could carry heavy loads from a short runway, the C-47 more than lived up to its nickname: Skytrain.

The C-47 was also one of the Army's most widely shared aircraft. The U.S. Navy designated it the R4D; the British Royal Air Force called it the Dakota; under a licensing agreement, the Russians built their own C-47s, which they called Lisunov Li-2s. Ironically, even the Japanese navy had their version, the L2D3, derived from DC-3 designs purchased prior to the war. But mostly, from the balmy Pacific Islands, to the blistering sands of North Africa, to the icy wastes of Alaska, the C-47 was the airplane that transported the American war

VITALS	
Designation	C-47B Skytrain
Wingspan	95 ft.
Length	64 ft. 5 in.
Max. Weight	33,000 pounds
Top Speed	232 mph
Cruising Speed	175 mph
Range	1513 miles
Ceiling	24,450 ft.

machine. When he wrote his memoirs, D-Day architect Dwight D. Eisenhower described the C-47 as one of the four most important weapons in winning the war, on par with the jeep, bazooka and atomic bomb.

The Douglas DC-3 aircraft, upon which the C-47 and its derivatives were based, rolled out on December 17, 1935. The militarized C-47 version, often referred to as the "Gooney Bird," had several enhancements, including a reinforced fuselage, stronger floors and large rear doors for loading cargo and dropping paratroopers. Powered by a pair of trusty Pratt & Whitney 1200-hp radial engines, the C-47 remained in production from January 1942 until the end of the war, in the summer of 1945.

The C-47 required a three-man crew: a pilot, copilot and navigator. Cabin accommodations were Spartan—most of the planes were outfitted with simple metal seats for 28 fully armed troops. A set of large cargo doors on the rear fuselage allowed a 37mm cannon or even a Jeep to be wedged onboard for supply missions. Douglas designed the plane to carry a 5000-pound payload, but tales of loads far past the Gooney Bird's official limit were legion.

The sturdy C-47 airframe invited much experimentation. One plan fit a Gooney Bird with floats instead of landing gear. Another experiment converted an engineless C-47 into an assault glider; it proved more economical to use the cargo plane to tow a pair of Waco CG-4A invasion gliders, a com-

(continued)

Hundreds of Allied soldiers of the 12th Air Force peppered southern France (above) after jumping from C-47s during World War II. The French Riviera invasion was one of the opening salvoes of Operation Dragoon, which began on August 15, 1944.

C-47B Skytrain

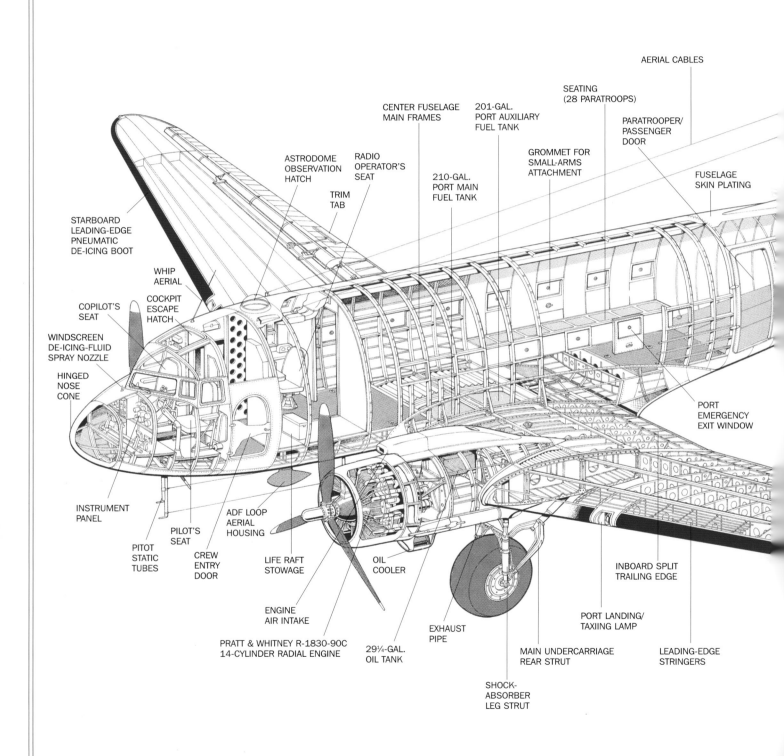

AERIAL CABLES

SEATING
(28 PARATROOPS)

CENTER FUSELAGE
MAIN FRAMES

201-GAL.
PORT AUXILIARY
FUEL TANK

PARATROOPER/
PASSENGER
DOOR

GROMMET FOR
SMALL-ARMS
ATTACHMENT

FUSELAGE
SKIN PLATING

ASTRODOME
OBSERVATION
HATCH

RADIO
OPERATOR'S
SEAT

210-GAL.
PORT MAIN
FUEL TANK

TRIM
TAB

STARBOARD
LEADING-EDGE
PNEUMATIC
DE-ICING BOOT

WHIP
AERIAL

COPILOT'S
SEAT

COCKPIT
ESCAPE
HATCH

WINDSCREEN
DE-ICING-FLUID
SPRAY NOZZLE

HINGED
NOSE
CONE

PORT
EMERGENCY
EXIT WINDOW

INSTRUMENT
PANEL

PITOT
STATIC
TUBES

PILOT'S
SEAT

ADF LOOP
AERIAL
HOUSING

CREW
ENTRY
DOOR

LIFE RAFT
STOWAGE

OIL
COOLER

INBOARD SPLIT
TRAILING EDGE

ENGINE
AIR INTAKE

EXHAUST
PIPE

PORT LANDING/
TAXIING LAMP

LEADING-EDGE
STRINGERS

PRATT & WHITNEY R-1830-90C
14-CYLINDER RADIAL ENGINE

29¼-GAL.
OIL TANK

MAIN UNDERCARRIAGE
REAR STRUT

SHOCK-
ABSORBER
LEG STRUT

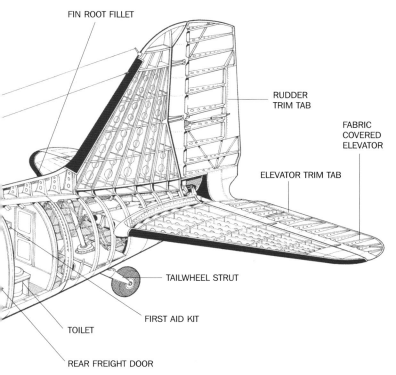

FIN ROOT FILLET

RUDDER TRIM TAB

FABRIC COVERED ELEVATOR

ELEVATOR TRIM TAB

TAILWHEEL STRUT

FIRST AID KIT

TOILET

REAR FREIGHT DOOR

bination used to varying degrees of success across several World War II theaters of operation.

The Army introduced the C-47's replacement, the quad-engine Douglas C-54 Skymaster, in 1944, but the existing fleet proved so durable that Gooney Birds remained in service for decades. C-47s played an important role in the Berlin Airlift, delivering supplies. And during Korea, they pulled double duty resupplying troops and serving as hospital planes. As soon as supplies were unloaded, a medical crew rigged the aircraft to carry 18 stretcher cases. During the battle at the Chosin Reservoir, C-47 crews evacuated 4689 casualties in five days.

Some of the C-47s still flying at the start of the Vietnam War were converted for reconnaissance missions, and others were equipped with automatic weapons and designated as AC-47 gunships. C-47s remained in service until 1975, when they were finally replaced by AC-119 and AC-130 gunships. The civilian DC-3, however, continues to fly for small airlines around the world. It also continues to amaze pilots with its durability, as it did on March 15, 2001, when a fire broke out in the No. 2 engine of a Jim Hankins Air Service DC-3 flying from Panama City, Florida, to Albany, Georgia. The engine dropped off and fell into a farmer's backyard, but the reliable plane was piloted safely to a nearby municipal airport.

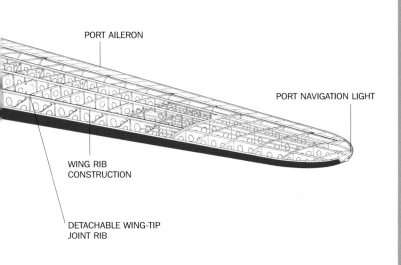

PORT AILERON

PORT NAVIGATION LIGHT

WING RIB CONSTRUCTION

DETACHABLE WING-TIP JOINT RIB

D-DAY

On June 6, 1944, as Allied troops stormed Normandy during the D-Day invasion, the first GIs to hit the beaches saw what at first appeared to be a massive gray cloud sweeping overhead from the west—an armada of 750 gliders pulled by a fleet of C-47 cargo planes.

Although the dawn landing had only begun, the glider assault was the second D-Day mission for these twin-engine aerial workhorses. Five hours earlier some 925 Douglas C-47s had begun to deliver 13,000 troops from the 82nd and 101st Divisions for what was considered the most difficult part of the D-Day operation: a massive night drop behind enemy lines. Although the invasion would prove the value of the C-47 as a combat as well as cargo aircraft, the airborne missions themselves would prove to be just short of disastrous. Cloud banks and flak scattered the C-47s so broadly that after the 6600 para-troopers of the 101st Airborne Division made their jumps, they found themselves too widely dispersed on the ground to be as effective a fighting force as mission planners had intended. The 82nd Airborne Division fared worse, with some 1500 of its men killed or captured and 60 percent of its equipment lost in swamps or dropped into fields covered by enemy fire.

The CG-4A rarely enjoyed such a picture-perfect landing (above); actual combat conditions were quite different. The Germans mined likely glider landing areas with linked explosives atop poles, a method glider pilots dubbed "Rommel's Asparagus." Additionally, hard landings in unfamiliar terrain reportedly caused the wheel struts to pierce the fuselage—a pointed hazard for strapped-in passengers.

CG-4A

Haig

• Waco

Essentially a winged freight car that got no respect, the "Bamboo Bomber" was the United States' most widely used disposable warplane.

The Waco CG-4A Haig, a glider designed to carry troops and weapons, was one of the most under-rated aircraft of World War II. Loaded to capacity, it could carry either 13 troops in full battle gear, or a jeep or quarter-ton truck, or a 75mm Howitzer. Haigs, known better as Hadrians as the British called them, were noteworthy not only for their size and weight-lifting prowess, but also for their manufacturing history. No fewer than 16 companies, including several with no prior connection to

the aviation industry, built more than 12,000 of these combat gliders. Ward Furniture built seven; Baldwin Piano produced parts. Oddly, the company that designed the boxy, wood-and-metal glider, Waco Aircraft Company of Troy, Ohio, built only about 1000. Nearly half of the production run were built by Ford Motor Company and Gibson Refrigerator.

The Hadrian was not a complex aircraft. Its wings were made of large sheets of plywood; the fuselage was a simple tubular metal frame covered with stretched cloth; and the cockpit, where two pilots sat side-by-side, was hinged to the top of the fuselage. One ingenious feature was a cable that ran aft from the nose, along the top of the cabin, then turned around a pulley and connected to the jeep or truck that was being transported—after a successful landing, the vehicle would drive out, pulling the cable and causing the cockpit to rise. In a crash this same arrangement could save the pilots' lives by very rapidly lifting them clear of the forward-shifting load.

A Hadrian made a less than graceful touchdown on a dirt field in the early 1940s (above). With its hinged nose lifted, the cavernous glider could ferry even a small bulldozer, made specifically for aerial delivery and designed to carve out airstrips behind enemy lines.

The bravery of the men who piloted Hadrians is beyond question; however the success of their missions is another matter. The Hadrians' combat records are at best spotty, with their most illustrious moments occurring during and after the June 1944 D-Day landings in France. Pairs of gliders entered the combat zone pulled by tow lines attached to C-47-class aircraft. Over the target area, the glider pilot released his 300-ft. tether and relied on skill and luck to bring his passengers or cargo safely to earth. With the troops on the ground and the cargo rolled out, the gliders were abandoned, and it was up to the pilots to find their way back to England. If they landed behind enemy lines, they had to fight alongside the troops they transported or the units receiving their cargo. Pilots carrying infantry became infantry themselves; pilots delivering Howitzers learned to pass the ammunition.

Hadrian aviators who were captured by the Germans, however, often received a kind of social, if not military, promotion: The Germans viewed their captives as the equals of fighter and bomber pilots—a status that eluded the glider fliers on their bases in England, where they were considered less than full-fledged aviators, men as expendable as their aircraft.

And in a sense, the Army did treat its more than 21,000 glider pilots as expendable. Most were recruited from the ranks of aviation cadets who were waiting for an opening in military flight school and soldiers with previous flying experience. On paper, glider pilot training consisted of 60 hours in light aircraft, 30 hours in sailplanes and 60 more hours in the CG-4A combat glider. In practice, light-aircraft training meant pilots began making unpowered, dead-stick landings as soon as they had mastered the rudiments of takeoffs and turns. Engineless Piper Cubs often made do in place of genuine sailplanes, an unfortunate substitute for the trainees.

When the war ended, several thousand Hadrians packed in heavy wood crates awaited shipment to England. Having no future in civilian aviation, they met an ignominious end as war surplus. Many were purchased by American midwestern farmers, who proceeded to salvage their wood, turning the lumber from the packing crates into building blocks for barns and hunting cabins, and the gliders themselves into chicken coops.

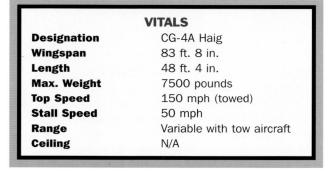

VITALS	
Designation	CG-4A Haig
Wingspan	83 ft. 8 in.
Length	48 ft. 4 in.
Max. Weight	7500 pounds
Top Speed	150 mph (towed)
Stall Speed	50 mph
Range	Variable with tow aircraft
Ceiling	N/A

When the Extender (above) reaches out with its telescoping boom, the Air Force's preferred refueling method, the aircraft on the other end can suck down 1100 gal. per minute. In its transport role the mighty KC-10, with a standard crew of four, can carry up to 75 personnel plus nearly 170,000 pounds of freight in 12,000 cu. ft. of cargo space. The first KC-10 flight was on July 12, 1980.

KC-10
Extender

• **McDonnell Douglas**

Thanks to these ingenious airborne service stations, the pilots of the armed services have never found it more easy to fill 'er up at 40,000 ft.

It is an understatement to say that aircraft fuel consumption has increased dramatically over time. The propeller-driven Boeing B-29 Superfortress carried about 8000 gal. of fuel. The 1950s-era Boeing B-47 Stratojet lugged 14,600 gal., while the Boeing B-52 Stratofortress tripled that capacity to more than 48,000 gal. A line of thirsty cars long enough to consume that much gasoline would extend more than nine miles.

Despite these large volumes, in-flight refueling is still a major enhancement to any aircraft's capability. Seaplanes can, of course, be landed alongside refueling ships. But sea takeoffs, which require engines running at maximum power and

VITALS	
Designation	KC-10A Extender
Wingspan	165 ft. 4 1/2 in.
Length	181 ft. 7 in.
Max. Weight	590,000 pounds
Max. Fuel Load	356,000 pounds
Speed	619 mph
Range	4400 miles fully loaded
Ceiling	42,000 ft.

depend upon Mother Nature to co-operate by providing flat seas, consume considerably more fuel than sustained flight at cruising speeds. It was clear, as aircraft design evolved, that an all-weather air force of an ambitious nation would need to master aerial refueling.

The Army had conducted an early experiment on August 25, 1923, in the skies over San Diego, California. During a 37-hour, 15-minute flight, two Air Service lieutenants successfully refueled their DH-4B Liberty 15 times. An even more impressive demonstration occurred six years later when an Air Corps Fokker C-2A named the Question Mark was refueled 42 times while setting a world flight-endurance record of 150 hours, 40 minutes, 14 seconds—an exercise that ended only because one of the plane's engines failed.

These impressive advances aside, in-flight refueling remained a tricky operation that depended largely on the refuelee pilot's skill, as he attempted to match speed and altitude with the tanker, catch and reel-in a flexible hose and securely attach it to his plane. This task was simplified with the debut of the "flying" boom in the late 1940s—a tele-scoping device operated by a tech-nician inside the tanker. Using a joystick-like controller that manipulated control surfaces on the end of the boom, the operator literally flew the pipe into a self-sealing receptacle on the aircraft in need of replenishment.

The McDonnell Douglas KC-10 Extender, which can fly up to 2200

miles from its home base, deliver 200,000 pounds of fuel and then fly home, is the most modern tanker operated by the U.S. Air Force. Selected for military service in 1977, it is based on the cargo version of the DC-10 jumbo jet.

Conversion of a DC-10F into a KC-10 begins with elimination of most upper-deck windows and lower-deck cargo doors. Seven fuel cells are installed below the main deck. Crew accommodations, including beds for the pilot, copilot, flight engineer and boom operator, are added to the cabin, along with military avionics, a fueling operator's work station and director lights to guide approaching aircraft. The KC-10 is also out-fitted with its own refueling receptacle, which enables it to join with another KC-10 or an older KC-135. Three General Electric CF6-50C2 52,500-pound-thrust turbofans provide the deep-welled tanker's power.

In the Gulf War, the KC-10 and KC-135 fleet performed 51,700 refueling operations, delivering some 125 million gal. of fuel to U.S. and coalition aircraft. The KC-10's projected service life of 30,000 hours means it could serve the U.S. Air Force until as late as the 2040s—making the Extender perhaps the most venerable American combat plane of them all.

From his special perch in the rear of the aircraft, the boom operator of a KC-10 (above) got up close and personal with an F-4 Phantom in April 1985. The action that adds to the Extender's name is controlled with a digital fly-by-wire system.

McDonnell Douglas AH-64 Apache

CHAPTER 7
Helicopters

The Sikorsky HH-60 Rescue Hawk (above) is a member of the Navy's Seahawk family. Armed with 7.62mm miniguns, it specializes in SEAL commando insertion and extraction as well as the recovery of downed aircrews. The chunky CH-47 Chinook (left) can carry 44 fully armed troops and has been a faithful tandem-rotor servant to the U.S. Army for nearly 40 years.

Helicopters

Once a dream of the great Leonardo da Vinci, the realities of the rotorcraft and of vertical flight have made invaluable contributions to every branch of America's armed forces since the Second World War.

One of the most important artifacts in the Smithsonian National Air and Space Museum hangs from the ceiling of the Paul E. Garber Preservation, Restoration and Storage Facility, a building rarely opened to the public. What's easily mistaken for the skeleton of a giant fan blade is actually a rotor from the H-1, a helicopter secretly built for the U.S. Army in 1921, some 20 years before Pearl Harbor. On December 18, 1922, the 3748-pound gangly creation rose hesitantly above what is now Wright-Patterson Air Force Base in Dayton, Ohio. In the months that followed, the H-1 logged 100 successful fights. While it never flew higher than

15 feet or remained aloft for longer than a few minutes, the H-1 conclusively proved that sustained vertical flight was possible. When the $200,000 test program concluded, the Army made a decision that defies explanation to this day; it ordered the H-1 destroyed. This questionable act may have been influenced by the brash personality of the H-1's inventor, George de Bothezat, an egotistical Czarist scientist who escaped to the United States following the Russian Revolution and once bragged, "I am the world's greatest scientist and outstanding mathematician!" This very combination of talents and bravado, however, may have

The new RAH-66 Comanche (foreground) locked rotors with an AH-64D Apache Longbow during an Army exercise. The reconnaissance/light-attack Comanche is still in development; its tank-killing Apache partner has already earned its stripes.

A Bell OH-58D Kiowa (above) with the Seventh Cavalry Regiment fired a 2.75-in. rocket during maneuvers. These armed observation helicopters helped protect international shipping from Iranian gunboats in the Persian Gulf during the late 1980s.

landing, hover and horizontal flight—in June 1922.

Compared to the rapid progress in fixed-wing flight that occurred during this period, the development of rotary-wing aircraft seemed at best slow and at worst destined for failure. The problem was not a lack of genius on the problem-solvers' parts but the sheer complexity of vertical flight itself. Before humans could grab this most elusive of aerial brass rings, a series of especially difficult conundrums had to be solved—not the least of which was that no one fully understood vertical-flight aerodynamics or how much power it required. Early experiments were guided purely by intuition, the product of the try, fail, try again approach that characterizes much of any industry's early forays into engineering.

Then there was the lack of a suitable source of energy. Early fixed-wing aircraft were essentially powered kites, which could become airborne with relatively little horsepower. The plane the Wright Brothers built for the Army, the Wright Military Flyer, had an engine of only 30.6 hp. By contrast, the feebly performing Army H-1 helicopter required a 230-hp engine to rise a mere 12 ft.

The dynamic forces acting on the airframe of the helicopter ruled out the use of wood and fabric, the materials of the day for fixed-wing aircraft design. Aluminum production had not yet reached the point where quantities needed for flight experimentation could be obtained affordably.

Once airborne, helicopters proved unstable for several reasons. One was the unequal lift created by the blades, depending upon whether they were moving with or against the relative wind. Additionally, helicopters required a mechanism to counteract rotor torque. Another Russian émigré, Igor Sikorsky, cleared this hurdle in 1940 with the now-familiar vertical tail-rotor design. And finally, the effects of vibration—still a factor to this day—caused a swift demise to many early airframes and rotors. Over time, these problems would be overcome; accordingly, the U.S. Army's interest in the helicopter would slowly rekindle, too.

In 1930, Arthur Young began a series of experiments that would encourage Lawrence Bell, founder of Bell Aircraft, to finance the development of the groundbreaking Model 30 prototype in

also enabled de Bothezat to succeed where dozens before him had failed.

From time immemorial, vertical flight had been the Siren's call of aviation. In principle, it appears as simple as duplicating the flight of a sycamore seed as it spirals in the wind. Toy helicopters, fashioned from a pair of feathers mounted at right angles to the top of a shaft, have mimicked this motion since 4th-century BCE China. Rolling the shaft through one's palms spins the feathers, causing them to bite into the air and rise. Centuries later Leonardo da Vinci and, more recently, the inventor Thomas Alva Edison attempted to apply the same principal to a man-size machine, but like so many others, the main problem with their designs was the lack of a sufficient powerplant.

The Army's interest in de Bothezat's approach was sparked by a flurry of activity in France in the summer and fall of 1907. In September a four-rotor machine designed by future aviation pioneer Louis Breguet—with the assistance of his university professor Charles Richet—lifted a pilot off the ground. Less than two months later another Frenchman, Paul Cornu, built a tandem-rotor flying aircraft that incorporated a rudimentary flight control system and reportedly made several short tethered flights.

According to historians at the Smithsonian Institution, however, credit for the first American true helicopter goes to the father-and-son team of Emile and Henry Berliner, whose creation demonstrated all the proper helicopter functions—vertical takeoff and

1941. Four years later, the legendary Bell Model 47 became the first helicopter to be certified by the Civil Aeronautics Board. It would go on to become the first commercially successful civilian helicopter and the Army's first practical helicopter, the H-13.

Although World War II spurred a far more rapid development of single and multiengine helicopters, the machines themselves had limited battlefield application. From a logistics perspective, these early craft were not cost effective, requiring a seemingly endless list of time-consuming safety checks and maintenance details. Pilots often described their helicopters as "1000 parts flying in close formation." From a combat perspective, the military value of the helicopter had yet to be defined. Initially, they were deployed as observation craft and, to a lesser degree, rescue craft. It was in this second role that helicopters would find their military footing in the Korean War. In concert with Mobile Army Surgical Hospitals, the MASH units immortalized by the namesake film and television program, MEDVAC helicopters would be credited with saving the lives of tens of thousands of young Americans. During the Vietnam War, the helicopter blossomed into both a troop transport and a gun platform. The Cold War saw rotary-wing aircraft's job description expanded to include the mantle of tank-killer.

Next on the horizon for the helicopter's evolution is a new type of craft—the tilt-rotor. Like a helicopter, it takes off and lands vertically, and it also hovers. Once airborne, however, its engines, mounted at the tips of stubby wings, can rotate 90 degrees, allowing the aircraft to fly like its fixed-wing cousins. A Bell-Boeing tilt-rotor designated the V-22 Osprey is the current front-runner to take over many of the helicopter duties of the U.S. Marine Corps.

A crewman eased a 2.75-in. rocket into an AH-1 HueyCobra's 19-rocket tube launcher (above) at the Cantho Airfield in South Vietnam's Mekong Valley on March 12, 1972. The gunship had just returned from a mission in support of South Vietnamese troops and took off again after rearming and refueling were completed.

Two U.S. servicemen stood under a Vietnamese sky filthy with Hueys. More than 5000 of the iconic Bell UH-1 Iroquois were deployed to South-east Asia. They will forever represent the Vietnam experience to a generation of Americans.

A line of Bell Model 47/H-13Ds (above) sat at the Niagara Falls Municipal Airport, awaiting transport to Korea in support of United Nations troops. The bubble-canopy choppers served the military in a variety of roles but gained the most fame for revolutionizing MEDVAC operations. Grateful wounded soldiers dubbed the H-13 the Angel of Mercy.

H-13
Sioux

• Bell

The first American commercial helicopter, which would go into service in 40 countries, the famed Bell Model 47 put the chop in choppers.

For many people around the world, the word helicopter brings the Bell Model 47 to mind. The image of a stretcher-bearing fishbowl-canopy helicopter settling into a swirl of dust at a Korean War-era Mobile Army Surgical Hospital has been permanently etched into our consciousness by the legendary television serio-comedy "M*A*S*H." By the Korean War, however, the Model 47 had been around for some time. Originally designed as a commercial helicopter, it made its first flight on December 8, 1945, and went into production the

following year. In the next 27 years, the Model 47 underwent 20 major model revisions; during this period, it would serve three branches of the U.S. military. More than 5000 Model 47s were eventually used in 40 nations, making it one of the world's most popular light-utility helicopters.

The H-13's roots go back to the Bell Model 30, an experimental helicopter that first flew in 1943. When the more capable Model 47A became available, the Army Air Forces purchased 28 for service testing in 1946. Ten were designated YR-13s, three YR-13As—meant for cold-weather service—and the remainder were transferred to the Navy and redesignated as HTL-1 trainers. In 1948 the U.S. Army purchased 65 Model 47s, which became H-13Bs, since the letter R for rotorcraft had been removed from the designation system. The official nickname Sioux was added later.

The H-13 was not the Army's first helicopter but would prove to be perhaps its most important, not only offering the Army new ways to fight, but also improving battlefield mortality rates by providing swift transport of wounded soldiers. In the Korean War the Army H-13 was used for observation and reconnaissance, but it was mostly known for missions popularized in "M*A*S*H": evacuating around 18,000 United Nations casualties and earning the nickname "Angel of Mercy." In the early days of the Vietnam War, it served chiefly as an observation platform, with some helicopters equipped with twin M37C .30-cal. or M60C 7.62mm machine guns.

The Model 47's success rested almost entirely with a brilliant designer named Arthur Young. Like many before him, Young had become obsessed with the idea of vertical flight. He began experimenting with helicopters in 1928, and in September 1941 he convinced the Bell Aircraft Corporation to finance two demonstration models. Young's breakthrough was the creation of the two-blade gyrostabilizer bar, which enabled the aircraft to remain stable without the complex arrangement of hinges on other experimental models. Mounted beneath the rotor, the short, weighted bar had streamlined counterweights at both tips.

A somber medical team (above) from the 8225th Mobile Army Surgical Hospital (MASH) took a break from patching up soldiers and posed in front of an H-13 MEDVAC helicopter on October 14, 1951.

Just as a toy gyroscope whirling in your hand resists changes to the angle of its rotating flywheel, Young's gyro-stabilizer bar kept a helicopter's rotor blades spinning in the same geometric plane despite sudden gusts of winds.

Young also exploited a flywheel's stored energy to make his helicopters safer, designing the Model 47 rotor system to amass enough energy to keep the rotor spinning in the event of an engine failure. In this condition of "autorotation" a helicopter could not gain altitude but would retain sufficient lift and enough control for the pilot to safely maneuver the craft to the ground. In flight, Young's stabilizer also made the distinctive "clop-clop" noise that first gave helicopters the nickname "choppers." The Model 47's powerplant was steadily improved over time. Many of the popular 47Gs were driven by Lycoming six-piston 280-hp TVO-435 engines.

The Model 47 not only pioneered widespread helicopter use but also helped blaze the trail to the moon. By coincidence the autorotation sink rate of the Navy's HTL-4 version of the Model 47 was similar to the descent rate of the Apollo Lunar Excursion Module. Special training with that particular helicopter gave astronauts a partial sense of what it would be like to land on the lunar surface.

Although most Model 47s have been replaced in air forces around the world, some of Arthur Young's precedent-setting choppers continue to make themselves useful as training craft.

VITALS	
Designation	H-13/Model 47G
Main Rotor Diameter	37 ft. 2 in.
Length	31 ft. 7 in.
Max. Weight	2950 pounds
Top Speed	105 mph
Max. Rate of Climb	990 ft. per minute
Range	247 miles
Ceiling	12,700 ft.

A British Royal Air Force Chinook (above) lit up its flare dispenser—which provides defense against ground fire and heat-seeking missiles—in dramatic fashion during equipment testing while on a humanitarian mission in Sierra Leone. The D model of the Chinook is an international favorite; over 600 are in service in air forces around the globe.

CH-47
Chinook

• Boeing

A Herculean hefter of Howitzers, ground troops, vehicles and more, the CH-47 is one of the world's foremost medium-lift helicopters.

During World War II the helicopter was a rare and temperamental beast. Like a bright but ornery teenager, it showed considerable potential but lacked reliability. In the early part of the Korean War, the H-13 demonstrated its potential in MEDVAC operations. Larger rotary-wing aircraft ferrying Marine and Air Force personnel would have been an obvious Army asset, but political bickering with the Air Force limited the Army to

only two chopper-equipped transport companies. As the Korean War dragged to stalemate, the transport helicopter's worth was made abundantly clear, and by June 1959, the Army had cleared a path toward selecting a new battlefield-mobility helicopter, the Vertol Model V-144, which sported two main rotors—instead of a vertically rotating smaller tail blade—to counteract the effects of torque on a helicopter's airframe. Three years

VITALS

Designation	CH-47D Chinook
Rotor Diameter (Each)	60 ft.
Length	51 ft.
Max. Weight	50,000 pounds
Top Speed	180 mph
Max. Rate of Climb	1522 ft. per minute
Range	265 miles
Ceiling	10,550 ft.

later, the Boeing-Vertol tandem-rotor helicopter entered service as the CH-47A.

The Chinook—as it was later named, like many Army helicopters, for a Native American tribe—is essentially a large open-bay fuselage suspended beneath a pair of meshing rotors. The Chinooks sent to Vietnam could ferry 44 fully equipped soldiers. The aft-mounted engines can work individually or in concert while driving the helicopter's two three-blade rotors. The improved CH-47D, powered by two Textron Lycoming T55-L-712 3750-shaft-horsepower (shp) turboshaft engines, debuted in 1982 and more than doubled the Chinook's payload to 25,000 pounds. The D model can also be refueled in flight. The newest Chinook, the all-weather MH-47E Special Operations Aircraft, features infrared imaging for low-altitude night missions and is optimized for covert troop insertion and extraction. Although the Chinook was originally designed to be unarmed, the MH-47E is also a fearsome fighter, thanks to window-mounted M2 .50-in. machine guns and Stinger missiles.

The Chinook's mandate traces back to the evolution of an oft-overlooked part of the air-power equation, Organic Army Aviation. The ability to use helicopters to swoop into an isolated area and quickly deploy troops was the obvious yin to the yang of early 1950s MEDVAC operations in which the H-13 had proved so successful. Yet, because of budget sniping between the Army and the newly independent U.S. Air Force, it was an opportunity left largely unexploited. The argument's root, however—a long-simmering dispute within the Army over the best way to use aircraft—predated the Air Force's establishment.

On one side was the highly visible and vocal General William "Billy" Mitchell, the godfather of strategic air power who believed that air resources were best deployed to disrupt an enemy's ability to wage war. This thinking would lead to increasingly heavier and longer-range bombers, faster fighters to defend them and, ultimately, the U.S. Air Force's inception in 1947.

On the other side were artillery commanders and their perception of the U.S. Army Air Corps' reluctance to assign aircraft and pilots to the highly dangerous task of looking down on battlefields and telling artillery batteries how to adjust their fire. In August 1940 the Army had begun experimenting with light aircraft to increase artillery fire efficiency. These "Grasshopper" aircraft proved so successful in maneuvers that less than two years later, the Secretary of War ordered observation aircraft integrated with the field artillery—making the aircraft an "organic" part of the operation.

Organic Army Aviation units, made up almost entirely of light, single-engine spotter aircraft, would evolve into today's largely helicopter-based multipurpose Army Aviation Branch, the service that has relied upon the CH-47 as an airborne pack mule for nearly 40 years.

A CH-47 delivered supplies (above) on a dusty morning. The Chinook also performs search-and-rescue aircraft recovery, fire fighting, disaster relief and MEDVAC operations, carrying up to 24 stretchers and two medical attendants, plus its standard crew of three

The Bell AH-1 Cobra was the first true helicopter gunship, setting the standard against which all future attack choppers would be measured. The addition of antitank weapons—with the the AH-1Q—strong enough to take out any Soviet battle tank began a major shift in the European armored-warfare equation. The AH-1T SeaCobra (above) is one twin-engine variant flown by the U.S. Marine Corps.

AH-1
Cobra

• **Bell**

An "interim" solution for armed escort choppers in Vietnam became a long-term asset and the military's first pure attack helicopter.

The Bell AH-1 modern attack helicopter traces its lineage to a MEDVAC helicopter conceived in 1955—before the Army was allowed to arm its helicopters—whose UH-1A designation became commonly pronounced as "Huey," the legendary chopper that would be built in larger numbers than any other western military aircraft since World War II.

Although the creation of the U.S. Air Force had technically stripped the U.S. Army of the airborne

ground-attack role, the Army began experimenting with arming their helicopters in 1956 at Fort Rucker, Alabama; the experience of Organic Army Aviation units during the Korean War had already hinted at the helicopter's enormous potential as a weapons platform. After much trial and error, the Army activated its first armed helicopter company in 1962. Based in Okinawa, it was assigned the mission of escorting helicopter transports.

That same year, the Pentagon formed the Tacti-

VITALS

Designation	AH-1F HueyCobra
Main Rotor Diameter	44 ft.
Length	44 ft. 7 in.
Max. Weight	10,000 pounds
Top Speed	140 mph
Max. Rate of Climb	1620 ft. per minute
Range	315 miles
Ceiling	12,200 ft.

The HueyCobra's varied fangs could be configured with 2.75-in. Folding Fin Aerial Rockets in 7- or 19-rocket tube launchers, a chin-mounted 7.62mm minigun, a 40mm grenade launcher and a 20mm automatic gun.

The Cobra continued to evolve with the addition of TOW antitank missiles. The Marine Corps ordered the twin-engine Bell variant AH-1J Sea-Cobra and, later, the vastly upgraded AH-1W SuperCobra. In 1989 the Army redesignated production Cobras to AH-1F, reflecting several previous upgrades in armament, avionics, transmission and cockpit. Its powerplant is an 1800-shp Textron Lycoming T53-L-703 turboshaft engine.

The Cobras of both the Army and the Marine Corps saw action in the Gulf War and took part in other U.S. military actions in the '80s and '90s. Additionally, modern Cobra variants have been sold to at least 10 foreign air forces around the world.

cal Mobility Requirements Board, which, after studying the results of a series of war games, recommended that the role of Organic Army Aviation be expanded to include not only transporting infantry and artillery but also providing local fire support. Three years later, the helicopter-based First Cavalry Division (Airmobile) was organized and put into combat in Vietnam, with the Huey as its principal helicopter.

When the Vietnam War shifted into high gear, Bell turned to their highly successful Huey to fill a requirement for an "interim" attack-helicopter while the Army awaited delivery of the Lockheed AH-56 Cheyenne. Bell's prototype, the Model 209, incorporated the powerplant, transmission and rotor of a UH-1B/C inside a new, slim fuselage—so thin, in fact, the pilot and gunner sat in tandem, in the rear and front seats, respectively. The rest of the machine was essentially devoted to weaponry, and thus was born the helicopter that the Army ordered into production as the AH-1G HueyCobra, a "quick-fix" so successful that it reportedly logged over a million hours in Vietnam. More than 1000 were built, and the Cheyenne program was eventually canceled.

A HueyCobra (above) buzzed a rocky hillside at low altitude. The tandem seating area of the svelte and deadly AH-1 is only 38 in. wide—a target area just over one-third that of the UH-1, the Cobra's famous and prolific progenitor.

AH-1S HueyCobra

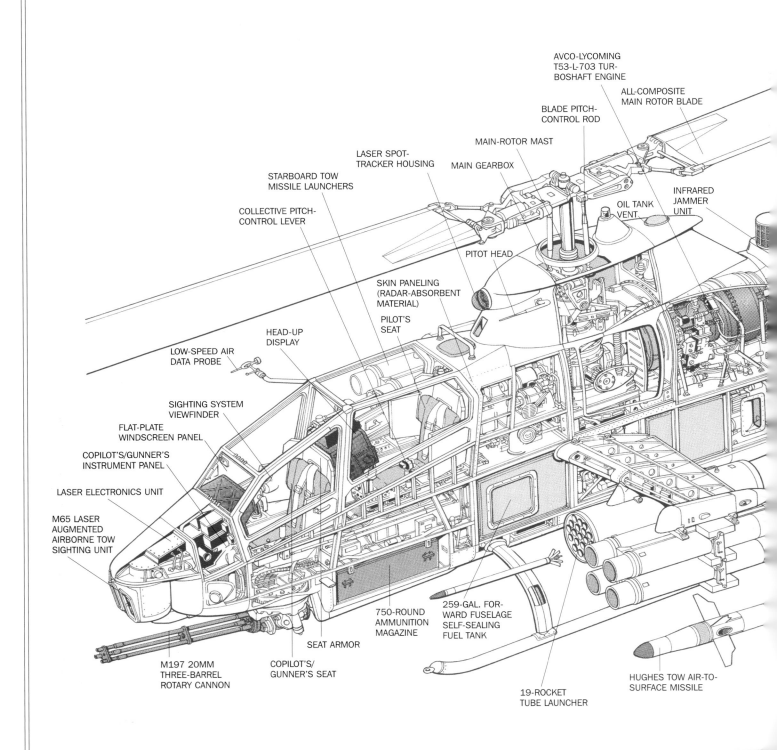

AVCO-LYCOMING T53-L-703 TUR-BOSHAFT ENGINE

ALL-COMPOSITE MAIN ROTOR BLADE

BLADE PITCH-CONTROL ROD

MAIN-ROTOR MAST

LASER SPOT-TRACKER HOUSING

MAIN GEARBOX

INFRARED JAMMER UNIT

STARBOARD TOW MISSILE LAUNCHERS

OIL TANK VENT

COLLECTIVE PITCH-CONTROL LEVER

PITOT HEAD

SKIN PANELING (RADAR-ABSORBENT MATERIAL)

PILOT'S SEAT

HEAD-UP DISPLAY

LOW-SPEED AIR DATA PROBE

SIGHTING SYSTEM VIEWFINDER

FLAT-PLATE WINDSCREEN PANEL

COPILOT'S/GUNNER'S INSTRUMENT PANEL

LASER ELECTRONICS UNIT

M65 LASER AUGMENTED AIRBORNE TOW SIGHTING UNIT

750-ROUND AMMUNITION MAGAZINE

259-GAL. FORWARD FUSELAGE SELF-SEALING FUEL TANK

SEAT ARMOR

M197 20MM THREE-BARREL ROTARY CANNON

COPILOT'S/GUNNER'S SEAT

19-ROCKET TUBE LAUNCHER

HUGHES TOW AIR-TO-SURFACE MISSILE

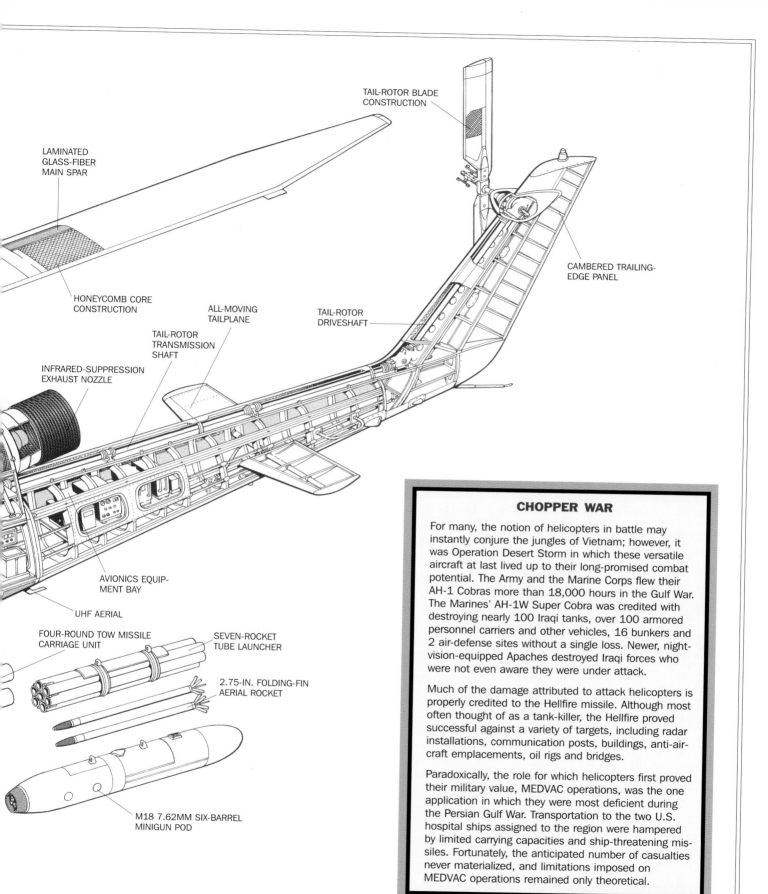

LAMINATED
GLASS-FIBER
MAIN SPAR

TAIL-ROTOR BLADE
CONSTRUCTION

CAMBERED TRAILING-
EDGE PANEL

HONEYCOMB CORE
CONSTRUCTION

ALL-MOVING
TAILPLANE

TAIL-ROTOR
DRIVESHAFT

TAIL-ROTOR
TRANSMISSION
SHAFT

INFRARED-SUPPRESSION
EXHAUST NOZZLE

AVIONICS EQUIP-
MENT BAY

UHF AERIAL

FOUR-ROUND TOW MISSILE
CARRIAGE UNIT

SEVEN-ROCKET
TUBE LAUNCHER

2.75-IN. FOLDING-FIN
AERIAL ROCKET

M18 7.62MM SIX-BARREL
MINIGUN POD

CHOPPER WAR

For many, the notion of helicopters in battle may instantly conjure the jungles of Vietnam; however, it was Operation Desert Storm in which these versatile aircraft at last lived up to their long-promised combat potential. The Army and the Marine Corps flew their AH-1 Cobras more than 18,000 hours in the Gulf War. The Marines' AH-1W Super Cobra was credited with destroying nearly 100 Iraqi tanks, over 100 armored personnel carriers and other vehicles, 16 bunkers and 2 air-defense sites without a single loss. Newer, night-vision-equipped Apaches destroyed Iraqi forces who were not even aware they were under attack.

Much of the damage attributed to attack helicopters is properly credited to the Hellfire missile. Although most often thought of as a tank-killer, the Hellfire proved successful against a variety of targets, including radar installations, communication posts, buildings, anti-aircraft emplacements, oil rigs and bridges.

Paradoxically, the role for which helicopters first proved their military value, MEDVAC operations, was the one application in which they were most deficient during the Persian Gulf War. Transportation to the two U.S. hospital ships assigned to the region were hampered by limited carrying capacities and ship-threatening missiles. Fortunately, the anticipated number of casualties never materialized, and limitations imposed on MEDVAC operations remained only theoretical.

In 1999 old hawk met new as a squat squadron of Sikorsky Black Hawks (above) recovered the wreckage of a Curtiss P-40E Warhawk where it had crashed in the Aleutians nearly 60 years earlier. An empty UH-60 can carry up to 8000 pounds suspended on a cargo hook. The extended Black Hawk family has been more than earning its keep since the prototype YUH-60 made its first flight in October 1974.

UH-60
Black Hawk

• **Sikorsky**

The best replacement for the UH-1 Huey imaginable, the Black Hawk has morphed into all things for all people in the U.S. military.

From time to time an aircraft comes along that is everything and more than the military expected, a platform that it can adapt to the challenge of new threats. The venerable Boeing C-47 Skytrain is perhaps the best example among fixed-wing aircraft, entering service in World War II and pulling varied military duties well into the Vietnam era. The UH-60 Black Hawk appeared destined to be a similarly robust craft almost immediately after it became operational.

Early in its involvement in Vietnam, the U.S. Army realized that it needed a troop transport that was faster and more survivable than the "Huey," the Bell UH-1 Iroquois. However, with the war in progress, formalization of the helicopter program that became known as UTTAS—Utility Tactical Transport Aircraft System—was delayed until 1972. With the war grinding down, and no future involvement for the Army on the horizon, a lengthy series of service tests began, pitting

VITALS

Designation	UH-60L Black Hawk
Main Rotor Diameter	53 ft. 8 in.
Length	50 ft. 1 in.
Gross Weight	24,500 pounds
Top Speed	183 mph
Max. Rate of Climb	1550 ft. per minute
Range	362 miles
Ceiling	19,140 ft.

Boeing-Vertol's YUH-61 against the YUH-60, designed by Sikorsky, the company founded by the legendary Russian-born helicopter pioneer. Sikorsky eventually won the competition, and in June 1979 the 101st Airborne Division took delivery of its first UH-60A Black Hawk.

Unlike the UH-1 Huey, which was conceived as a transport and was only later armed, the Black Hawk was designed for combat from the very beginning. It flies with a three-man crew, two on the flight deck and a loadmaster, who also serves as the door gunner. The helicopter's basic armament would eventually include a pair of .50-cal. machine guns or 7.62mm miniguns, mounted on either side of the forward cabin. Equipped as a transport, the UH-60A can carry an 11-man squad in addition to its three-person crew. With the rear cabin seats removed, it can transport as many as 20. Reflecting the fierce firefights helicopters were flown into during Vietnam, its fuel tanks were bulletproofed to offer an added margin of protection when Black Hawks touched down in "hot" landing zones. For swift, easy transport into war zones, the tail sections of the helicopter fold; one Black Hawk can squeeze into a C-130 transport, six can travel aboard the giant Air Force C-5A Galaxy.

Today, the Army operates two basic transport versions of the Black Hawk: the UH-60A and an improved UH-60L, which is powered by two General Electric T700-GE-401C 1880-shp engines and can add extra fuel tanks or hardpoints for up to 16 Hellfire missiles via a detachable external stores system.

The basic H-60 design has proved capable for a host of other missions. For MEDVAC, the specially equipped UH-60Q can ferry as many as six stretchers. Special operations MH-60 Pave Hawks, have forward-looking infrared radar, terrain-following radar and a refueling probe for extended operations. The HH-60G Night Hawk is modified for Air Force rescue operations. CH-60 Seahawks fulfill many roles for the Navy, including antisubmarine warfare and search-and-rescue. And the U.S. Marine Corps' nine VH-60N White Hawks—decked out with additional soundproofing and deluxe seating—are the swank airborne limousines for the President of the United States.

Both the A and L Black Hawks are scheduled for upgrades under the UH-60X program. Among other improvements, they will receive even better engines and new avionics, ensuring that these remarkably durable helicopters will continue serving the Army on all fronts for years to come.

A lone soldier (above) descended from a Black Hawk during Special Operations maneuvers in 1999. Black Hawks have assisted the U.S. armed forces in actions from Grenada to Bosnia and almost everywhere in between. The Black Hawk also serves the U.S. Coast Guard, Customs Service and over 20 friendly foreign governments.

AH-64
Apache

• McDonnell Douglas

A tank-buster that proved its mettle in the Gulf War, the Apache gunship will fulfill Army attack roles well into the 21st Century.

Throughout the Cold War, the United States committed itself to maintaining a sufficiently strong military to achieve victory in two simultaneous conflicts. The Vietnam theater, dominated by jungle canopy, had focused a considerable amount of the Army's attention on the value of helicopters. But there was also the potential for classic tank warfare, which could have broken out if the Soviet Union had decided to invade western Europe. Such a scenario, the Pentagon reasoned, would likely begin with a massive armored campaign.

To address many threats, the Army wanted a fast, all-weather tank-killing attack helicopter that could operate day or night. Bell, maker of the AH-1 Cobra, and Hughes Aircraft were asked to develop prototypes. The Army selected the Hughes

In missions against light armored vehicles, the Apache (above) can pack up to 76 2.75-in. Folding Fin Aerial Rockets; reloading on the ground takes just ten minutes. Its Hellfire rockets can penetrate the armor of any known battle tank. Its transmission—traditionally a weak point in helicopter design—is machined so precisely that the Apache can run for up to an hour after losing its entire supply of oil.

YAH-64A entry in December 1976 but did not immediately place a large production order. Instead, it asked for four more test models. Over the next five years, the original design underwent significant changes, including major redesigns of the rotor and tail structures as well as the addition of an infrared-suppression device to help mask the heat generated by the two turboshaft engines. The first production order for 11 helicopters was placed in 1982, and the first aircraft was delivered in January 1984, coincidentally the month that Hughes became part of McDonnell Douglas.

The tank-killer Apache is something of a tank in its own right: Most of its critical flight control systems were designed to survive a hit by a 23mm projectile; the lower half could sustain fire from 12.7mm weapons; and the two-man crew is protected by lightweight boron shields. The AH-64 is also the most crashworthy helicopter yet built. Tests showed there was a 95 percent chance the gunner, who sits in front, and the pilot, behind and 19 in. above him, could survive if their aircraft hit the ground at just over 28 mph.

Adding to the Apache's versatility is that the helicopter can avoid detection by adjusting its altitude to fly in what is referred to as "ground clutter," a region where low structures, trees and other natural features reflect radar, making it nearly impossible to discriminate among stationary and moving objects. "Nap-of-earth" flight this close to the ground is challenging

The Apache's cockpit (above) was a focal point of anti-armor activity during the Gulf War. With the Longbow upgrade, the Apache reportedly can identify over 128 targets, pick out the 16 deadliest, transmit the data to other aircraft and attack within 30 seconds.

in the daytime; at night it requires a special forward-looking infrared system that identifies obstacles in the flight path by their thermal signatures.

Apache units distinguished themselves in the Persian Gulf, hitting two Iraqi radar sites on January 17, 1991, with the first air-launched shots of Operation Desert Storm. After the sand had settled on the final ground offensive, AH-64s were credited with destroying hundreds of tanks and other vehicles.

Despite its fine weapons, the Army has experienced some difficulties in adapting to post-Cold War logistical conditions: When Apache units were sent to support United Nations intervention in Kosovo, it took three weeks and 16 full mission rehearsal exercises before crews were ready for action. Among the snags: Few of the pilots were trained to fly with night vision goggles, under high-tension power lines or in the area's Alpine-like gorges.

The Army has begun to replace its fleet of Apache AH-64As with the improved AH-64D Apache Longbow, powered by two 1890-shp General Electric T700-GE-701C turboshafts. One of the chief upgrades is the Longbow radar, which is integrated with the helicopter's avionics and its powerful Hellfire missiles. Most current Hellfire missile systems require a target to be "painted," usually by a laser emanating from an assisting aircraft, like an OH-58 scout. With the new system, the Apache commander will be able to select a range of targets and launch missiles in a "fire-and-forget" mode.

VITALS

Designation	AH-64D
Main Rotor Diameter	48 ft.
Length	49 ft. 2 in.
Max. Weight	22,283 pounds
Top Speed	162 mph
Max. Rate of Climb	214 ft. per minute
Range	1180 miles
Ceiling	13,690 ft.

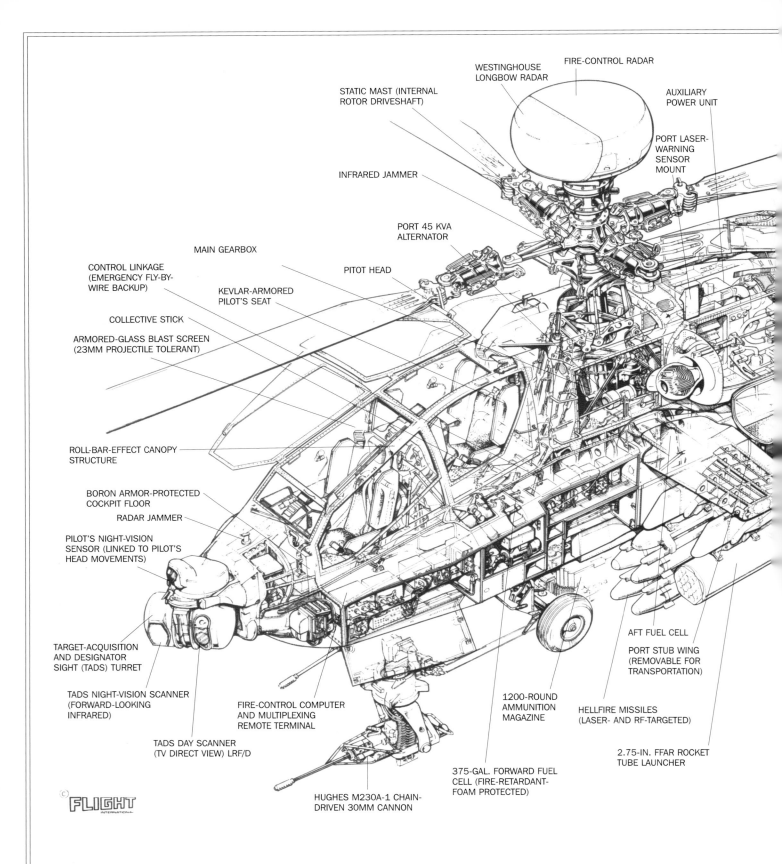

WESTINGHOUSE LONGBOW RADAR

FIRE-CONTROL RADAR

STATIC MAST (INTERNAL ROTOR DRIVESHAFT)

AUXILIARY POWER UNIT

PORT LASER-WARNING SENSOR MOUNT

INFRARED JAMMER

PORT 45 KVA ALTERNATOR

MAIN GEARBOX

PITOT HEAD

CONTROL LINKAGE (EMERGENCY FLY-BY-WIRE BACKUP)

KEVLAR-ARMORED PILOT'S SEAT

COLLECTIVE STICK

ARMORED-GLASS BLAST SCREEN (23MM PROJECTILE TOLERANT)

ROLL-BAR-EFFECT CANOPY STRUCTURE

BORON ARMOR-PROTECTED COCKPIT FLOOR

RADAR JAMMER

PILOT'S NIGHT-VISION SENSOR (LINKED TO PILOT'S HEAD MOVEMENTS)

TARGET-ACQUISITION AND DESIGNATOR SIGHT (TADS) TURRET

TADS NIGHT-VISION SCANNER (FORWARD-LOOKING INFRARED)

TADS DAY SCANNER (TV DIRECT VIEW) LRF/D

FIRE-CONTROL COMPUTER AND MULTIPLEXING REMOTE TERMINAL

HUGHES M230A-1 CHAIN-DRIVEN 30MM CANNON

375-GAL. FORWARD FUEL CELL (FIRE-RETARDANT-FOAM PROTECTED)

1200-ROUND AMMUNITION MAGAZINE

AFT FUEL CELL

PORT STUB WING (REMOVABLE FOR TRANSPORTATION)

HELLFIRE MISSILES (LASER- AND RF-TARGETED)

2.75-IN. FFAR ROCKET TUBE LAUNCHER

AH-64D Apache Longbow

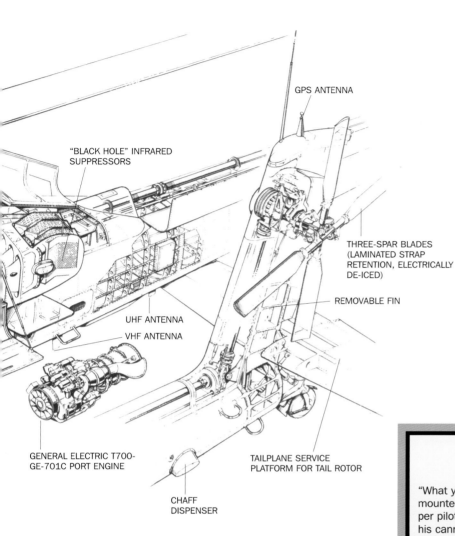

GPS ANTENNA

"BLACK HOLE" INFRARED
SUPPRESSORS

THREE-SPAR BLADES
(LAMINATED STRAP
RETENTION, ELECTRICALLY
DE-ICED)

REMOVABLE FIN

UHF ANTENNA

VHF ANTENNA

GENERAL ELECTRIC T700-
GE-701C PORT ENGINE

TAILPLANE SERVICE
PLATFORM FOR TAIL ROTOR

CHAFF
DISPENSER

IN PM'S WORDS
The Look That Kills

"What you see is what you hit. With a new helmet-mounted gunsight developed by Honeywell, all a chopper pilot has to do is look at an enemy target and fire his cannon. The cannon instantly lines up on the target, automatically following his line of sight no matter which way he moves his head.

"The heart of this remarkable system is a tiny, transparent eyepiece attached to the pilot's helmet so that it covers his right eye. The eyepiece is electronically coupled to a servo-driven optical scanner held in a movable gimbal mount in the aircraft's nose. The scanner, either a TV camera for daylight use or an infrared sensor for night vision, follows the movements of the pilot's head, looking wherever he looks. The cannon, located under the nose in a similar gimbal mount, is servo-slaved to the scanner so it points wherever the scanner is aimed.

"What the pilot sees superimposed on the eyepiece is a brightly defined view of the terrain below, even in bad weather or darkness, making it easy to pick out a target that might otherwise be invisible. Also displayed in the eyepiece is vital flight information, such as heading, speed and altitude, so the pilot can fly the craft without having to look down at his instruments."

—Sheldon Gallager
POPULAR MECHANICS, February 1985

RAH-66
Comanche

• **Boeing-Sikorsky**

Designed for the combat engagements of tomorrow, this futuristic, lethally armed spy chopper is the world's most advanced helicopter.

By the early 1980s the U.S. Army's leadership was envisioning a new kind of helicopter, one that was optimized for both reconnaissance and attack missions and harkened back to the small-unit approach to combat in Vietnam. Subsequently, the Army's Light Helicopter Experimental Program was undertaken in 1982. By 1988 the project's form was sufficiently clear that the Pentagon requested proposals from two competing teams, Bell-McDonnell Douglas and Boeing-Sikorsky, whose design for the RAH-66 Comanche was selected in 1991. The Soviet Union's collapse had proved the Pentagon's

point; the Comanche would be a new weapon to police the low-intensity conflicts of an emerging new world order. Its first flight was January 4, 1996.

Army Chief of Staff General Gordon R. Sullivan describes its mission: "Comanche will be the eyes and ears of the commander on the lethal future battlefield. It must deploy rapidly, see without being seen and inform commanders at many levels. If necessary, the Comanche must influence the battle with organic weapons—precision strike—and at times, the Comanche crew must control the maneuver battle . . . ."

The RAH-66 Comanche (above) made its first flight in 1996. A stowable 20mm Gatling gun and a fully retractable missile armament system contribute to its low radar cross-section and help make the combined missions of attack and reconnaissance possible. The agile Comanche also redefines evasive action: It can pull off a snap turn in 4.5 sec. and fly backward at a zippy 80 mph.

First and foremost, the Comanche would replace and combine the roles of the Army's existing fleet of AH-1 HueyCobras and Bell OH-58 observation helicopters. Those combat choppers represent 30-year-old technology and limited tactical abilities and are rendered inoperable in night combat, bad weather, high altitude or hot environments, or in situations where nuclear, biological or chemical weapons might be used. And, like all Army helicopters, they require extensive maintenance. The Comanche will address these shortcomings and add substantial capabilities.

The Comanche (above) displayed its striking eight-blade shrouded tail rotor as it was eased into a C-17 Globemaster III, on the way home from a first appearance outside the United States, at the 1998 Farnborough International airshow.

One of the strictest requirements for this new helicopter is the speed with which it must move to the action. The Comanche can, in the Pentagon's language, "self-deploy." It has to be ready to fly to a battle area at least 1200 miles from its base and land with a 30-minute fuel reserve. On the ground, its crews have a limit as short as 15 minutes to refuel it, arm it with Stinger or Hellfire missiles, and reload the ammunition for its chin-mounted 20mm three-barrel General Electric Gatling gun. For more distant operations, where the RAH-66 would have to arrive by a military transport, it will need just 45 minutes before heading into the fray.

The types of fast-strike operations that the Comanche would fight would require the aircraft commander to quickly adapt to a rapidly changing battlefield. To accomplish this, the Comanche is equipped with a "Tactics Expert Function," a sort of video game in which all the tactical information available to a mission commander—local topography, position of friendly and hostile forces, etc.—is loaded into the Comanche's on-board computers; before takeoff, the commander would do a "practice" fly-through of the difficult areas of the mission. Information would be updated as the Comanche flies into actual combat, making last-minute changes possible. The RAH-66 would also transmit reconnaissance data to the battlefield commander and coordinate the attack.

While the Comanche is not a stealth aircraft, its basic design helps to minimize its presence: The airframe creates a small radar cross-section; a low-glint canopy reduces reflected light, making the helicopter less visible by day; and an exhaust-gas-cooling system coupled with the Comanche's two 1432-shp T800-LHTEC-801 turboshafts make it less visible to infrared detectors at night. Its combat systems not only detect enemy radars but can also plan routes around them.

With the program still in development, the Comanche's combat record is unwritten. Two prototypes are undergoing tests, six more helicopters are scheduled to be built in 2001, and the Comanche should be operational in 2006. For those old enough to recall the beginnings of Organic Army Aviation, when helicopters were curious flying pack mules, the sleek Comanche promises a new golden age of armed helicopters.

VITALS	
Designation	RAH-66 Comanche
Main Rotor Diameter	39 ft. 1 in.
Length	42 ft. 10 in.
Max. Weight	17,408 pounds
Top Speed	201 mph
Max. Rate of Climb	1418 ft. per minute
Range	1338 miles with external fuel tanks
Ceiling	20,000 ft.

F-14 Tomcat on the deck of the _USS John F. Kennedy_

The Grumman C-2 Greyhound (above)—an aerial cargo aircraft that resupplies the floating cities known as aircraft carriers—is one of the hardest working cargo airplanes in the skies. During a normal assignment, two C-2s will log around 1000 hours, transport about 5000 people and move approximately 1 million pounds of cargo. Its payload capacity is 10,000 pounds.

Wings of the Navy

U.S. naval aviation has enjoyed a long, proud tradition of defending American interests in all theaters of warfare, via aircraft carriers, land-based airfields and—in specialized seaplanes—the ocean itself.

When European naturalists reached the Australian continent they encountered animals like the koala, which looked familiar from the outside but was actually remarkably different from any creature they had ever seen. A similar observation might be made about the aircraft operated by the United States Navy. The fighters that catapult off the flight decks of aircraft carriers may appear identical to those lifting off from airfields, but under their skins they are very different animals indeed. Naval aircraft also differ in a broader, historic sense. Army and Air Force aviation evolved along a similar technological path, from biwing to mono-

plane, open cockpit to closed flight deck, piston engine to jet engine. In contrast, U.S. naval aviation saw the evolution of four very different types of flying machines: seaplanes, airships, and conventional fixed- and rotary-winged craft.

Naval aviation arrived at its present heading by following an indirect course. Initially, the Navy saw aircraft as the airborne eyes of the fleet. An early naval flying boat, the Curtiss HS-12, flew antisubmarine patrols on the U.S. coastline, and it became the first American plane to see combat when a British flier piloting an HS-12 with the Royal Navy Air Service sank a German U-boat in

Two crewmen inspect a four-seat Grumman EA-6B Prowler. The electronic-warfare variant of the A-6 Intruder, the Prowler played a prominent role in the jamming and destruction of enemy radar during Operation Desert Storm.

The 1930s-era Curtiss F9C-2 Sparrowhawk (above) represented a brief, ill-fated foray into launching combat planes from dirigibles—hence the fearsome hook mounted in front of the cockpit. The Grumman S-2C Tracker (right), which first flew in 1952, was the first aircraft designed purely for the Navy's antisubmarine carriers. It carried a torpedo and six rocket racks.

September 1917. A champion of seaplane development, the Navy teamed with Curtiss to produce the NC-4, which, in May 1919—eight years before Charles Lindbergh's nonstop trans-Atlantic flight—flew from Newfoundland to Lisbon, making only one stop along the way.

Beginning in the 1920s, the Navy became a leading force in exploiting the military potential of the airship. The *Akron* ZRS-4, a rigid, helium-filled airship longer than a battleship, was literally a flying aircraft carrier. Packed amid the *Akron*'s gas bags—the source of her buoyancy—were tiny Curtiss F9C Sparrowhawks that could be launched and recovered from a true flying trapeze that dangled beneath the airship's belly. Although the era of the airborne aircraft carrier would end tragically with the weather-related crashes of the *Akron* and her sister ship, the *Macon*, in 1933 and 1935, respectively, smaller, non-rigid air vehicles, or blimps, continued to play a role in antisubma-

rine warfare through the early Cold War years.

The Navy took a more conservative approach in developing conventional floating aircraft carriers. More than two decades passed between Eugene Ely's first takeoff in a 50-hp Curtiss biplane from a temporary flight deck constructed on the cruiser *Birmingham* in 1910 and the 1933 launch of the *USS Ranger* (CV-4), the first ship actually designed and built as—not converted to—an aircraft carrier. Any doubts about the value of naval aircraft vanished following the seminal World War II battles of the Coral Sea and Midway Islands. In the years that followed, a tamer application of the nuclear power that so dramatically ended the Second World War revolutionized naval power. On-board nuclear reactors eliminated the necessity for small fleets of fueling vessels, the chief logistical obstacle to maintaining an armada at sea. On land, American reactors generated enough electricity to power a small city. The United States now had the ability to apply force

almost anywhere in the five oceans' vast expanse.

From the very beginning of jet aviation, the Navy was at the forefront of experimentation. Aircraft manufacturers quickly adapted airframes to accommodate the rapid acceleration of catapult launches and the corresponding deceleration of arrested landings. Fighters, attack planes, bombers and helicopters (which resupplied naval aircraft and became a valued search-and-rescue tool) were all hardened for the rigors of life at sea.

As the aircraft carrier was refined into the crown jewel of the Navy's fleet, its nemesis, the submarine, was also vastly improved. When he solved the fundamental problems of submarine design, father of the modern submarine John Holland also created a means of stealthily delivering one of the 20th century's first terror weapons, the torpedo. As late as World War II the term "submarine" remained something of a misnomer. In practice, these craft were actually low-draft surface vessels that dipped beneath the sea to attack. Only later, when they were powered by nuclear reactors, did they approach the undersea capabilities of Jules Verne's fictional vessel, the *Nautilus*.

However, naval aviation put considerable effort into destroying these silent, underwater ship-killers. The ability of seaplanes and airships to lift keen-eyed observers, radar and metal detectors high above the water transformed the feared German Wolf Packs from the hunters to the hunted. Today, anti-submarine warfare remains one of naval aviation's more important, and dangerous, missions. The young men and women who were briefly held hostage in April 2001, after their Lockheed EP-3 ARIES II was damaged by a hot-dogging Chinese pilot and forced to make a perilous emergency landing on Hainan Island, were on a mission that their grandfathers who had fought in World War II could well understand: They were, in all likelihood, listening for signals of Chinese submarines in the South China Sea.

Since the 1950s the Pentagon has pressured the Navy to adopt aircraft with more "commonality" with those flown by the Army and Air Force. The Joint Strike Fighter program, which aims to create a multiservice combat airfleet, may indeed achieve this goal. Regardless of the types of aircraft the Navy flies into the future, the contribution of naval aviation to the nation's defense will remain an indelible part of our American heritage.

The Lockheed EP-3 ARIES (Airborne Reconnaissance Integrated Electronic System) II (above) is the Navy's only land-based signals intelligence (SIGINT) spyplane. In addition to its state-of-the-art submarine-tracking sensors, the ARIES II can carry the Harpoon air-to-surface missile, the MK-50 torpedo and the MK-60 mine. Its airframe is based on the P-3 Orion.

The Lockheed S-3A Viking combined the peculiarities of antisubmarine aircraft with the power of jet speed—its General Electric TF34 turbofans consumed comparatively small amounts of fuel at low altitudes, allowing the Viking to hunt its prey for up to 7 ¹/₂ hours.

Although considered obsolete by many experts in 1939, the PBY Catalina (above) became the most relied upon flying boat of the Second World War. Approximately 4000 of the seaplanes were built from 1936 to 1945. Postwar Catalinas served in more than a dozen foreign air forces; the last U.S. Navy PBY-6A Catalina was retired in January 1957.

PBY
Catalina

• Consolidated

A flying boat almost written off by the Navy would prove to be one of the most prized and valiant naval assets of the Second World War.

Napoleon is reputed to have said that every infantryman carries the general's baton in his pack. This sentiment would prove applicable to the humble PBY Catalina, one of the most important naval weapons of World War II.

In the 1930s the United States Navy was still unconvinced of the utility of aircraft carriers. It focused its aviation efforts on perfecting coastal patrol aircraft that could take off and land at sea.

Conceived in 1933 and intended to replace the Martin P3M and Consolidated PY-series patrol boats—the Navy's first single-wing seaplanes—the Catalina patrol-bomber represented the Navy's third generation of seaplanes. The PBY was designed by the brilliant aeronautical engineer Isaac Maclin Laddon, who broke impressive technical ground with his creation. With the innovative use of internal wing bracing, Laddon was able to remove most external struts and all wire bracing. This reduced drag and enabled early PBYs to carry their bomb loads over 1200 miles. The first PBYs delivered in 1937 were pure flying boats that had to be towed to shore for repairs. Two years later the addition of retractable tricycle-style landing gear made the Catalina a true amphibian.

Although the PBY could hit hard, it was slow and could not take a punch—two of the most important requirements for an airborne warrior. At a time when fighters maxed out at hundreds of miles per hour, the Catalina sauntered along at a stately 117-mph cruising speed. A more serious shortcoming was the plane's equivalent of a boxer's glass jaw. The PBY had no armor to protect its aircrew and lacked self-sealing fuel tanks, which meant a lucky shot could turn the flying boat into a flying torch. The Navy was tempted to discontinue the PBY in 1939; history, however, had other plans.

America's investment in a more advanced flying boat would pay off for the European governments that were searching for any type of aircraft they could use to counter the long ignored, but newly manifest threat of Nazi Germany. So production of the PBY ramped up for both the U.S. Navy and the Lend-Lease program. The improved PBY-5, delivered in 1940, was powered by two Pratt & Whitney Twin Wasp 1200-hp engines and defended itself with two .30-cal. and two .50-cal. machine guns. Some

It took several brave men to coax the best from the PBY Catalina (above). The crew consisted of three pilots, a plane captain/head mechanic, two radiomen, two ordnance men and several machinist mates. The flying boat came complete with a tiny galley, several bunks and a portable sit-down toilet.

self-sealing fuel tank protection was added as well.

Despite its early shortcomings, the PBY would play a role in the three legendary naval engagements of World War II, and it would achieve the distinction of sinking more tonnage of Japanese shipping than any other aircraft in the Pacific war.

The Lend-Lease arrangement provided both equipment and technical expertise, and in May 1941 an American instructor copiloting a PBY with the British Royal Air Force spotted the pocket-battleship *Bismarck*. The Royal Navy would sink the massive German vessel the next day, killing more than 2000 sailors. Later that year, a PBY would make the only attack on a Japanese vessel—a midget submarine—just prior to the Pearl Harbor attack. Initiating the Battle of Midway in June 1942, a PBY made the first sighting of the Japanese invasion forces. The finest hours for the PBY would come with the merger of two new technologies, radar and magnetic anomaly detectors (MAD). Painted black to hide in the night sky, the PBY "Black Cats" squadrons carried out a series of surprise nighttime raids that sank hundreds of tons of enemy shipping. MAD-equipped "Mad Cat" Catalinas also identified and sank enemy submarines.

By war's end, more than 4000 of the not-quite-perfect patrol-bombers had contributed more to the Allied effort than anyone could have predicted.

VITALS	
Designation	PBY-5 Catalina
Wingspan	104 ft.
Length	63 ft. 10 in.
Max. Weight	34,000 pounds
Top Speed	189 mph
Cruising Speed	110 mph
Range	2545 miles patrol
	1500 miles tactical
Ceiling	17,000 ft.

PBY-5A Catalina

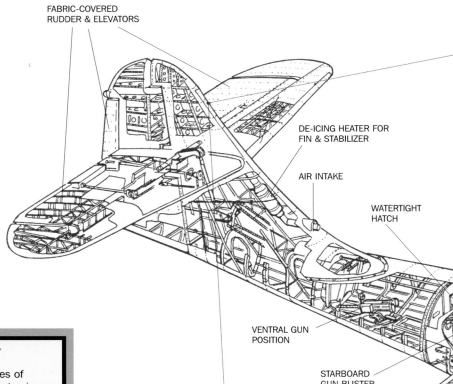

FABRIC-COVERED
RUDDER & ELEVATORS

DE-ICING HEATER FOR
FIN & STABILIZER

AIR INTAKE

WATERTIGHT
HATCH

VENTRAL GUN
POSITION

STARBOARD
GUN BLISTER

MAIN SPAR

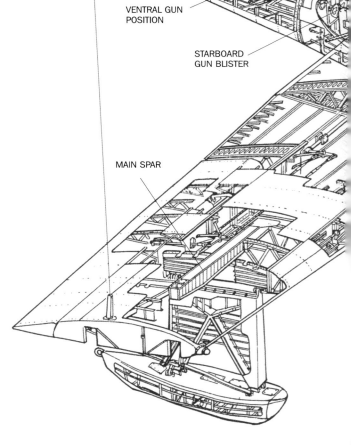

THE BATTLE OF MIDWAY

A PBY Catalina struck the first blow in a series of events that led to the most decisive five minutes in naval combat history, the Battle of Midway.

American aircraft carriers had escaped the attack on Pearl Harbor; a confrontation between the carrier forces of the United States and those of Japan was inevitable. The showdown came off the Midway Islands, selected by Japanese Admiral Isoruku Yamamoto, whose Combined Fleet steamed from Tokyo toward the pivotal U.S. base in late May 1942.

What Yamamoto did not know was that his naval codes had been broken. The U.S. carriers *Enterprise*, *Hornet* and *Yorktown* were hastily dispatched to destroy Yamamoto's carrier strike force.

In the early hours of June 4, four Navy PBYs pinpointed the looming invasion fleet and attacked Japanese transports; the flying boats sank an oiler before heading for home. Later that day, torpedo-bomber attacks from the three American carriers were smothered by Japanese Zeroes. However, the fighters had been distracted enough for a swarm of dive-bombers from the *Enterprise* to swoop down and fatally damage Japan's carriers *Kaga*, *Akagi* and, later, *Hiryu*. Sorties launched from *Yorktown* hit the *Soryu*, which was later sunk by a U.S. submarine.

Devastated, the Japanese fleet retreated the next day. The definitive naval battle of World War II had been won not by ships, but by aircraft.

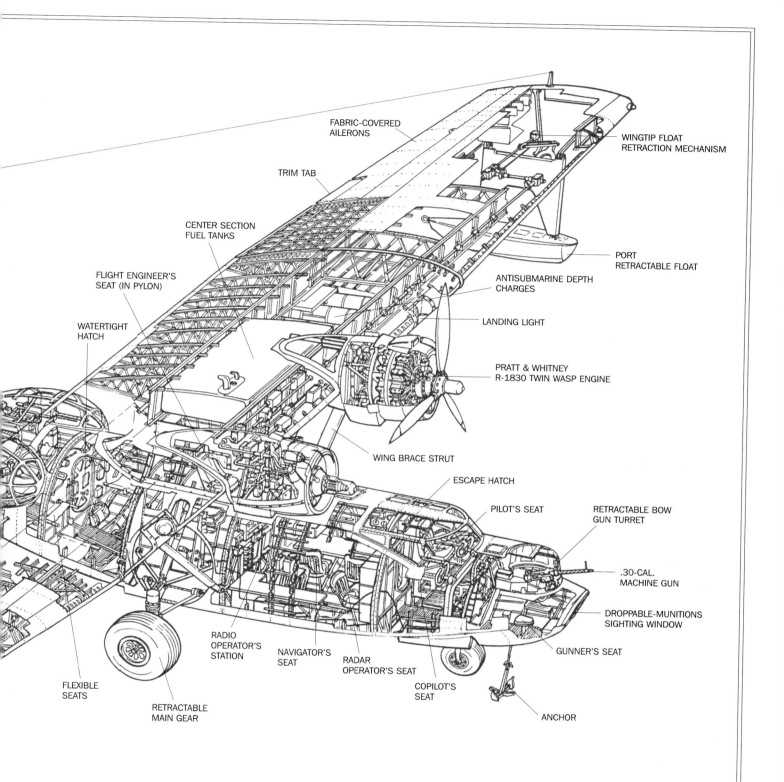

FABRIC-COVERED
AILERONS

WINGTIP FLOAT
RETRACTION MECHANISM

TRIM TAB

PORT
RETRACTABLE FLOAT

CENTER SECTION
FUEL TANKS

ANTISUBMARINE DEPTH
CHARGES

FLIGHT ENGINEER'S
SEAT (IN PYLON)

LANDING LIGHT

WATERTIGHT
HATCH

PRATT & WHITNEY
R-1830 TWIN WASP ENGINE

WING BRACE STRUT

ESCAPE HATCH

PILOT'S SEAT

RETRACTABLE BOW
GUN TURRET

.30-CAL.
MACHINE GUN

DROPPABLE-MUNITIONS
SIGHTING WINDOW

RADIO
OPERATOR'S
STATION

NAVIGATOR'S
SEAT

RADAR
OPERATOR'S SEAT

GUNNER'S SEAT

FLEXIBLE
SEATS

COPILOT'S
SEAT

RETRACTABLE
MAIN GEAR

ANCHOR

The F4U Corsair (above), with its massive tri-blade propeller, jauntily sloped wings—which reduced drag where they joined the fuselage—and smooth "spot-welded" skin, made its first flight as the XF4U-1 in May 1940. The combination of the more than 2800-cu.-in. 1850-hp Double Wasp engine and the Hamilton Standard Hydromatic prop made the Corsair the first naval fighter to exceed 400 mph.

F4U
Corsair

• Vought

A Navy hand-me-down to the U.S. Marine Corps survived relentless tinkering, stretched its gulled wings and rose to the occasion.

In 1938 the U.S. Navy Bureau of Aeronautics issued a requirement for an ambitious aircraft that pressed beyond the realm of existing engine, airframe and landing-gear technology. The resulting plane would become the fastest and highest flying carrier-based aircraft of World War II, the Vought F4U Corsair.

The Corsair was initially designed around the most reliable aircraft engine available in the United States, the Pratt & Whitney R-1830 Wasp air-cooled radial engine. Two years later, however, the speed-obsessed Navy demanded a faster plane, and Vought redesigned the aircraft with the then experimental Pratt & Whitney R-2800 Double

VITALS	
Designation	F4U-4 Corsair
Wingspan	41 ft.
Length	33 ft. 8 in.
Gross Weight	14,670 pounds
Top Speed	447 mph
Cruising Speed	215 mph
Range	1560 miles
Ceiling	37,000 ft.

Wasp. The most powerful engine in the world at the time, it had 18 cylinders that generated more than 100 hp each—about as much as the entire engine of a modern compact car. To take advantage of the Double Wasp's 1850-hp output, designers specified a tri-blade Hamilton Standard Hydromatic propeller. At 13 ft. 4 in., it was astoundingly large for a fighter and capped what amounted to a deal-breaker of a problem for naval aviation: The Vought F4U Corsair could not perform the single most important task required of a modern naval aircraft—a safe landing on an aircraft carrier.

When a plane touches down on the deck of an aircraft carrier, its tailhook is caught by a steel cable connected to a dampening mechanism that arrests the plane's forward motion. To withstand the shock of landing, and prevent a plane from jumping out of this "trap," the landing gear must be short and strong. Since the plane's cockpit was placed far aft, and its front end raised high so that the prop could clear the deck, a Corsair's pilot could neither see well during takeoff nor make out the instructions of the Landing Signals Officer during landing. This visual nightmare was exacerbated by chronic oil and hydraulic leaks that smeared the windscreens. Landings often ended in disaster when the planes bounced and slipped free of the arresting wire.

The Navy—whose pilots dubbed the new fighter the "Ensign Eliminator"—determined the F4U was unsuitable for sea-based operations and gave it to the Marine Corps. Land-based Marine aviators, however, took full advantage of the

heavy armaments of the 2450-hp F4U-4 to riddle ground positions in support of invasion landings. With the aid of six, wing-mounted .50-cal. machine guns (or four 20mm cannons) and two 1000-pound bombs or eight 5-in. rockets, the Navy's "Ensign Eliminator" became the Marines' "Sweetheart of Okinawa."

The British Navy, which was pleased to have any additional aircraft, was undaunted by the visibility problem. To solve windscreen smearing it wired down the cowl flaps across the top of the engine. The more difficult problems of aligning the plane for a carrier landing and then keeping it in the "trap" were solved by modifying the approach to incorporate a low, swooping curve rather than a direct, high-angle descent, enabling pilots to keep the signal officer in view as their planes cleared the fantail.

Encouraged by what the British had done, the U.S. Navy—which had been ordering design refinements all along and flying land-based Corsair squadrons since 1943—resumed carrier trials with the F4U in April 1944, but sea-based operations would not commence until January 1945, when the Marines Corps Corsairs flew from the USS Essex.

The resilient F4U would go on to exceed the Navy's initial lofty goals. By the war's conclusion, American Corsairs had flown nearly 65,000 sorties and shot down over 2000 Japanese aircraft; more than 12,500 of the gull-wing fighters had been built for the United States and other allied powers.

Corsairs flew long after World War II, as well. In the 1950s the F4U-4 (above on the USS Leyte) would fly interdiction missions against the North Koreans; French F4U-7 fighters would not be decommissioned until the mid-1960s.

While the Curtiss SB2C Helldiver (above) was faster, heavier and larger than the Douglas SBD Dauntless, its handling left something to be desired, and extensive modifications were required before a production aircraft made its maiden flight in June 1942. Less than five months later, a Helldiver squadron flying from the *USS Bunker Hill* made an attack on Rabaul, New Britain, in the South Pacific.

SB2C
Helldiver

• Curtiss

The last of the two-place dive-bombers—known as the "Big-Tailed Beast"—the Curtiss SB2C Helldiver was a true flying piece of work.

One year before the Second World War ignited in Europe, the United States was still in the grip of the Great Depression and loathe to become embroiled in the crisis in Europe. Yet, despite the prevailing woes at home, the U.S. Navy was in a curiously enviable position. Isolationism and distant saber rattling had underscored the importance of the Navy's essentially defensive mission, since 1935, to protect American shores, and funding for naval aviation was more readily available despite a period of budgetary restraint. To that end, naval planners had been busily developing long-range patrol aircraft and two-place dive-bombers— which evolved into SB-class scout-bombers—since

VITALS

Designation	SB2C-4 Helldiver
Wingspan	49 ft. 9 in.
Length	36 ft. 8 in.
Gross Weight	16,287 pounds
Top Speed	295 mph
Cruising Speed	158 mph
Range	1235 miles
Ceiling	29,100 ft.

The combat record of the SB2C is mixed. Fifty SB2Cs took off to fight against the Japanese Navy in the First Battle of the Philippine Sea, but only five returned. Most were ditched by their pilots after running out of fuel. Helldiver fliers reported that the SB2C was very difficult to control during carrier-landing approaches and "reinterpreted" the dive-bomber's designation as the "Son-of-a-Bitch Second Class." Some joked that the planes would better serve the war effort as ship anchors.

Conversely, Helldivers proved tremendously successful in a raid on Rabaul, when a single squadron sank a pair of cruisers and a destroyer. In raids on Truk, that same squadron lost only one aircraft, while destroying 176,000 tons of Japanese shipping. Additionally, Helldivers contributed to the destruction of two of Japan's largest warships, the *Musashi* and the *Yamato*. Later, the SB2C's reputation with the French navy in Indochina would be more uniformly favorable.

Inspired, perhaps, by Germany's success with dive-bombers during the Spanish Civil War, the Army attempted to adapt the SB2C for land attack. Under the designation A-25A, the retooled Helldiver could deliver 2000 pounds of bombs over a

(continued)

the late 1920s. And in 1938 the Navy had great expectations for a new Curtiss design, with an innovative internal bomb bay and the promise of high performance.

The five-year delay, however, between the Navy's decision to develop the SB2C and the date that the first combat-worthy Helldiver saw action reflected the difficulty of designing carrier-based aircraft. In February 1941, two months after its first flight, the XSB2C prototype crashed during a final approach. That December, a rebuilt prototype suffered the most basic of dive-bomber defects when it crashed after one of its foldable wings fell apart in a test dive. Fortunately, both the test pilot, who parachuted to safety, and the SB2C program survived the mishap. Then a new set of problems emerged during carrier-landing tests: Either the gear assembly failed on contact or the plane bounced away from the arresting cables. Designers were forced to go back to the drawing board. In all, over 800 changes were made before the Navy was satisfied with its production aircraft, the third Curtiss plane to carry the moniker Helldiver.

Most models were powered by a Wright 1900-hp 14-cylinder air-cooled engine. The plane's weapons included four .50-cal. wing-mounted guns and two flexible .30-cal. machine guns in the observation position. Underwing racks and the internal bay could deliver up to 2000 pounds of bombs; later versions also carried eight 5-in. rockets.

An SB2C Helldiver (above) banked toward an aircraft carrier while returning home after a raid against a Japanese warship on June 1, 1945. The Helldiver proved its worth during the final two years of the war.

SB2C-1C Helldiver

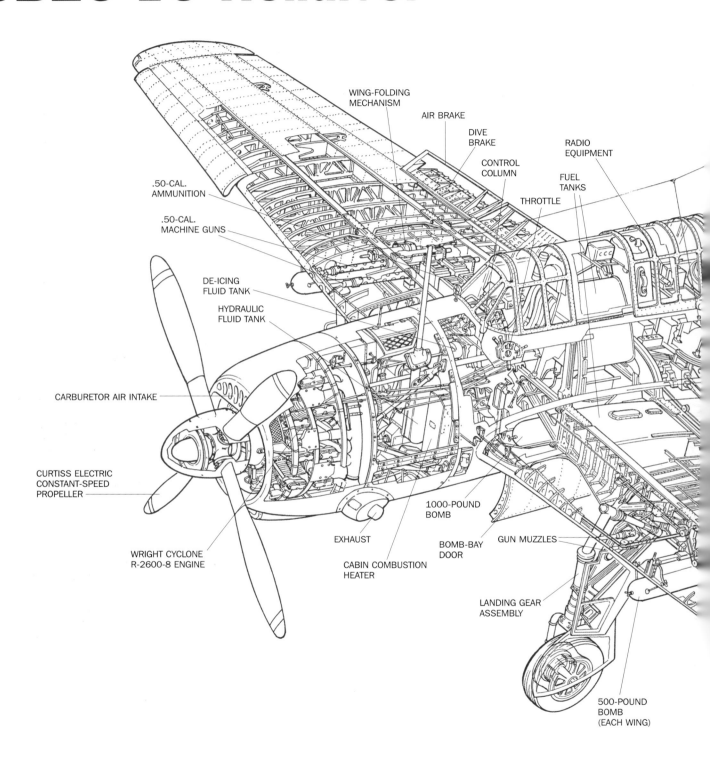

WING-FOLDING
MECHANISM

AIR BRAKE

DIVE
BRAKE

RADIO
EQUIPMENT

CONTROL
COLUMN

FUEL
TANKS

THROTTLE

.50-CAL.
AMMUNITION

.50-CAL.
MACHINE GUNS

DE-ICING
FLUID TANK

HYDRAULIC
FLUID TANK

CARBURETOR AIR INTAKE

CURTISS ELECTRIC
CONSTANT-SPEED
PROPELLER

WRIGHT CYCLONE
R-2600-8 ENGINE

EXHAUST

1000-POUND
BOMB

BOMB-BAY
DOOR

GUN MUZZLES

CABIN COMBUSTION
HEATER

LANDING GEAR
ASSEMBLY

500-POUND
BOMB
(EACH WING)

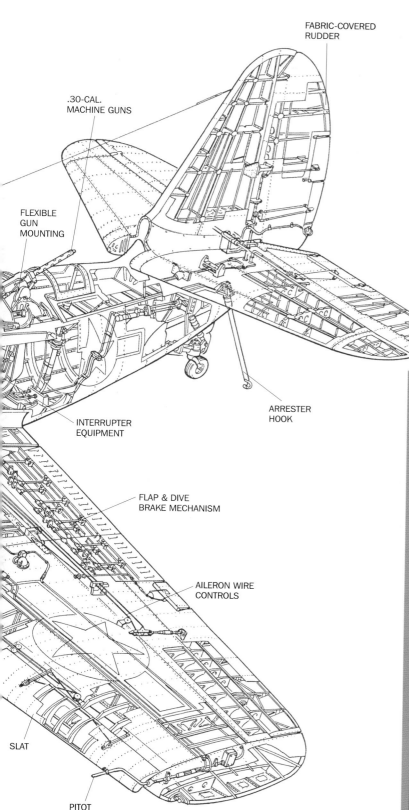

FABRIC-COVERED RUDDER

.30-CAL. MACHINE GUNS

FLEXIBLE GUN MOUNTING

INTERRUPTER EQUIPMENT

ARRESTER HOOK

FLAP & DIVE BRAKE MECHANISM

AILERON WIRE CONTROLS

SLAT

PITOT HEAD

1000-mile range. The converted plane never saw combat, however; the USAAF decided to replace its two-seat bombers with single-seat versions, and the A-25 was assigned to restricted duty as a training aircraft.

The controversial Helldiver will always have both proponents and critics. Only one of the more than 7000 SB2C variants built is reportedly in flyable condition, unlike the North American P-51 Mustangs that are lovingly preserved by the hundreds; however, the Helldiver's status as the standard dive-bomber for the U.S. Navy in every battle during the last year of World War II is incontrovertible. In sheer numbers alone, the SB2C Helldiver struck the Japanese more than any other warplane.

IN PM'S WORDS
Our Flying Navy

"You're clutching the stick of a training plane wobbling through what looks like a serene sky but feels like a condemned roller coaster. Down below there is the blue but terrifying ocean, at its edge the Pensacola air school where you hope some day to win the coveted Wings of the Navy.

"Instructions pour into your gosport helmet in a confusing fog. No chance to ask questions. Scarcely time to keep up with commands.

"'Bring the nose up!'

"Your mind flashes back to the text book, bounces swiftly back to business as directions come from the instructor. You maneuver the stick with a tense fist, find the left wing dropping, finally coax it level again.

"'Try it again.' Over and over, for forty minutes, and your first flight ends. You can grin now. It wasn't so easy as it looked from below, when you saw that flight of trim, twin-motored seaplanes roaring overhead in perfect geometrical formation; but it was a thrill, the first on the road to that ultimate in thrills: the receiving of Navy Wings. You're on your way to becoming one of the 8,000-odd young fellows who in a little more than a quarter century have proved themselves mentally, physically and psychologically sound enough to complete the flight training course at the U.S. Naval Air Station."

—J.B. Hancock
POPULAR MECHANICS, June 1940

The tandem-rotor Boeing CH-46 Sea Knight (above) buzzed the scrubby eastern tip of Vieques Island, Puerto Rico, broadcasting bilingual messages that warned of incoming practice rounds from the destroyer *USS Stump* on May 10, 2000. The Sea Knight has performed a variety of services for Navy and Marine forces since its first deployment to South Vietnam in 1965.

CH-46
Sea Knight

• **Boeing**

The intermeshing twin rotors of the hardy Sea Knight have flown and ferried the Few and the Proud for more than a generation.

Because the U.S. Marine Corps fights on land, it is easy to forget that it is actually part of the Department of the Navy. When Marines are called upon for ground assault, however, they fulfill a different function from both the Army, with which they employ common weaponry and equipment, and special forces units, with which they often share tactics. The Marines are America's expeditionary forces—the oldest branch of the military services and, after 200 years, still the point of America's

spear when it is necessary to project power to the most distant points on the globe.

While the Army, including special forces units, is based within the United States, the Marines keep an expeditionary force at sea that travels with naval forces and allows them to react rapidly to threats on land. Given their mandate to arrive first and apply force at critical choke points, it is hardly surprising that the Marines gravitated toward the helicopter as the perfect vehicle for carrying them

VITALS	
Designation	CH-46E Sea Knight
Rotor Diameter (Each)	50 ft.
Length	44 ft. 7 in.
Max. Weight	24,300 pounds
Top Speed	165 mph
Max. Rate of Climb	1715 ft. per minute
Range	152 miles (land-assault)
Ceiling	12,800 ft.

into harm's way. Depending upon several variables, Marines can deploy from ship to shore in amphibious troop carriers, in hovercraft and by air, which, for nearly half a century, has meant a brief ride aboard a Boeing CH-46 Sea Knight helicopter.

The Sea Knight is closely derived from the Vertol Model 107, which flew for the first time in April 1958. Interest in adapting this tandem rotor, medium-lift helicopter for military purposes had initially come from the Army, which purchased three for evaluation but rejected them in favor of the larger Boeing CH-47 Chinook.

At that time, the Marines relied upon the Sikorsky CH-34, a piston-engine helicopter developed for the Navy's antisubmarine warfare program and later adapted as a civilian passenger and military troop transport. The complex transmission and controls of a helicopter have always made it inherently prone to mechanical failure, and the piston engines of the day tended to introduce a further level of unreliability. Marines, like many soldiers who flew helicopters, were eager to trade up to more reliable jet powerplants.

From their experiences with troop-transport helicopters in Korea, the Marines also recognized the advantages of the tandem-rotor configuration, which created a wide cargo bay that could be rapidly loaded and unloaded. This was vital for the Marines, as they

are particularly likely to be met by hostile enemy action upon landing.

The Marines selected the Sea Knight as their assault-transport helicopter in 1961, and the following year the first model took to the air. Deliveries commenced in 1964, a year before the United States began to expand its involvement in Vietnam. Within four years, Sea Knights had logged 75,000 hours, during which they flew 180,000 missions and carried half a million troops.

Between 1964 and 1971 Boeing provided over 620 Sea Knights to the Marines and Navy, which continues to use them for on-ship personnel and supply delivery. Over 300 of the helicopters remain in military service. Upgrade programs have added more powerful engines, cambered rotor blades and larger fuel sponsons, among other improvements. The current CH-46D/E models rely on a powerplant of two 1870-shaft-hp General Electric T58-16 engines.

The Sea Knight's combat role fills a special niche. To establish a beachhead, Marines typically deploy AH-1 attack helicopters and Harrier jets to provide cover, while the unarmed Sea Knight ferries about 18 Marines at a time from ship to shore.

Until 2001, the Marine Corps had planned to phase out its CH-46 helicopters as it phased in the Bell-Boeing V-22 Osprey tilt-rotor; the Osprey, however, has been plagued with crashes. Whether the faithful Sea Knights will be put to pasture or carry the Marines well into the 21st century remains, so to speak, up in the air.

Three Marines clung to a hillside as three CH-46 Sea Knights ferried a company of their compatriots (above) during a training mission. The Sea Knight has a crew of three and can carry about 18 troops or 15 stretchers and two medical attendants.

USS
Abraham Lincoln (CVN-72)

In a time of national crisis the top brass almost always asks one question first: Where are the carriers?

A modern aircraft carrier is an airport built on top of a floating city. It is as well-equipped as any small-town community in America, complete with automatic-teller machines and different places to eat. About 5700 people live on a Nimitz-class aircraft carrier, like the *USS Abraham Lincoln* (cutaway below). Roughly 3200 of these men and women comprise the ship's company, which cooks the meals, washes the clothes and performs the thousand-and-one tasks that make any large enterprise a success. Their job is to support the work done by their 2480 comrades in arms, the members of the flight wing.

Together, these dedicated souls make it possible for the carrier to perform its three-fold mission: to provide deterrence in peace, a mobile air base in moments of crisis and a floating fortress during times of war.

The flight deck is the center of the action. When the captain—by tradition a naval aviator—orders the carrier turned into the wind, this unyielding field of steel becomes one of the busiest places on earth. Aircraft, armed and dangerous, arrive from below deck by elevators large enough to move a two-family house. Wings unfolded, the jets take their place at one of two side-by-side catapults at the ship's bow or at two waist catapults during staggered takeoffs. Afterburners glowing, the planes are shot off the deck by a blast of steam.

Landing on a carrier has been compared to a controlled crash. With the throttle set for a touch-

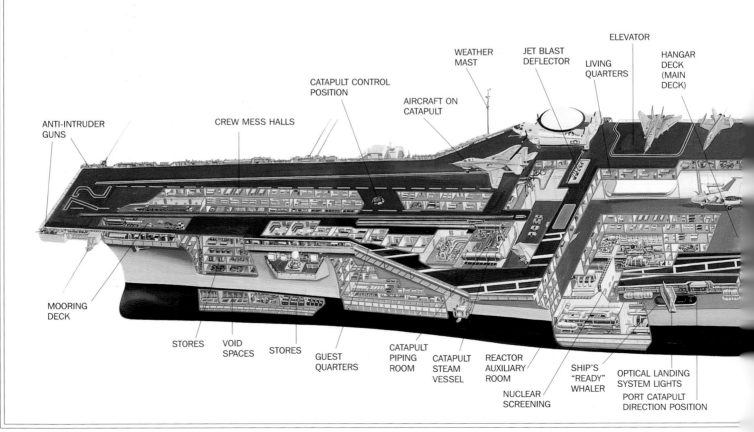

ANTI-INTRUDER GUNS

CREW MESS HALLS

CATAPULT CONTROL POSITION

AIRCRAFT ON CATAPULT

WEATHER MAST

JET BLAST DEFLECTOR

LIVING QUARTERS

ELEVATOR

HANGAR DECK (MAIN DECK)

MOORING DECK

STORES

VOID SPACES

STORES

GUEST QUARTERS

CATAPULT PIPING ROOM

CATAPULT STEAM VESSEL

REACTOR AUXILIARY ROOM

NUCLEAR SCREENING

SHIP'S "READY" WHALER

OPTICAL LANDING SYSTEM LIGHTS

PORT CATAPULT DIRECTION POSITION

Nimitz-class carriers like the *USS Abraham Lincoln* (above) are the largest warships in the world. Their evaporators distill more than 400,000 gal. of water per day.

and-go landing, the pilot aims for a contact point that will cause the tailhook beneath his aircraft to catch one of the aft steel cables—the same kind that hold up small bridges—that stretch across the deck. An arresting mechanism halts the plane's forward motion. And so it continues, hour after hour, day after day, in fine weather and foul, as carrier pilots practice the profession of peacekeeping.

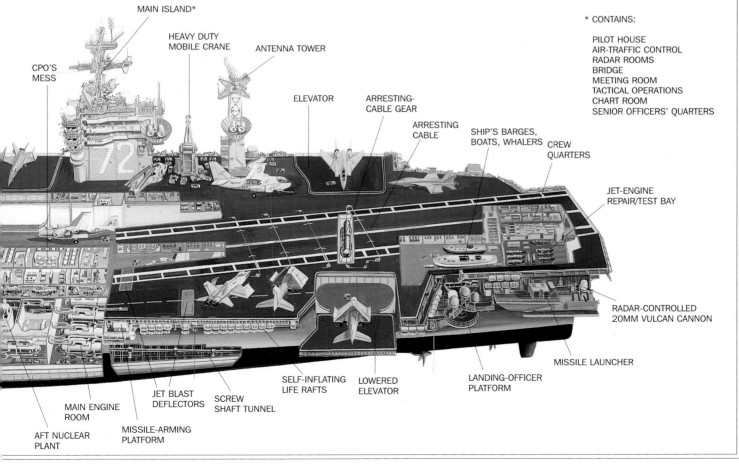

MAIN ISLAND*

HEAVY DUTY
MOBILE CRANE

ANTENNA TOWER

CPO'S
MESS

ELEVATOR

ARRESTING-
CABLE GEAR

ARRESTING
CABLE

SHIP'S BARGES,
BOATS, WHALERS

CREW
QUARTERS

JET-ENGINE
REPAIR/TEST BAY

RADAR-CONTROLLED
20MM VULCAN CANNON

MISSILE LAUNCHER

LANDING-OFFICER
PLATFORM

SELF-INFLATING
LIFE RAFTS

LOWERED
ELEVATOR

JET BLAST
DEFLECTORS

SCREW
SHAFT TUNNEL

MAIN ENGINE
ROOM

MISSILE-ARMING
PLATFORM

AFT NUCLEAR
PLANT

* CONTAINS:

PILOT HOUSE
AIR-TRAFFIC CONTROL
RADAR ROOMS
BRIDGE
MEETING ROOM
TACTICAL OPERATIONS
CHART ROOM
SENIOR OFFICERS' QUARTERS

The Grumman A-6 Intruder (above) was a legendary hauler of munitions, precision or otherwise. "You could have hung two barn doors out there and it still would go 480 knots," former A-6 pilot and retired Rear Admiral Charlie Hunter said of the famous combat plane. The wide-shouldered Intruder could carry up to 18,000 pounds of bombs or a cornucopia of air-to-ground and air-to-air missiles.

A-6
Intruder

• Grumman

The Navy's bulbous bomber was an attack plane that refused to quit, sometimes flying barely 200 ft. above the ground in horrendous weather.

The introduction of jet-powered Soviet MiGs during the Korean War made the U.S. Navy's piston-engine planes obsolete in an instant. After the war, when the Navy set down specifications for its first jet-powered, long-range, low-level attack aircraft, it drew on the lessons the U.S. Air Force had learned flying attack missions in Korea. Specifications for the new aircraft required the ability to hit small targets at night and in inclement weather.

The winning proposal—there were 11 competing companies—became the Grumman A-6 Intruder, the Navy's principal attack aircraft in Vietnam. It would play a significant role in every major U.S. military engagement that followed, including the Gulf War. In the 1970s, the Intruder would become the basis for the EA-6B Prowler, a stretched, four-seat variant, which would become the Navy's standard carrier-borne electronic-warfare aircraft.

The A-6 was neither fast nor sleek. The cruising speed of the A-6E—the most advanced Intruder, built around a pair of Pratt & Whitney J52-P-8B engines that each generated a modest 9300 pounds of thrust—was slower than most commercial airliners. Its refueling probe, which protrudes in front of the plane's canopy and angles upwards toward the plane's blunt nose, looks as if it might have fallen off another aircraft and grafted itself to the unsuspecting Intruder. The plane's echelon seating—unusual for a high-performance combat plane—placed the pilot and weapons officers side-by-side and not in tandem.

The A-6's pack-mule beauty and relative pokiness may be exactly what the Navy intended all along. Instead of afterburners, the initial A-6 aircraft sported tailpipes that could swivel downward to shorten takeoffs and landings. (When later tests showed that diverting jet thrust would slow the aircraft by only 7 mph, the idea was abandoned.) Looks and speed notwithstanding, the A-6 was a fly-anywhere-anytime aircraft that could beat an enemy into submission with a load of 500-pound iron bombs, a brace of laser-guided missiles or three nuclear weapons.

One of the Intruder's most striking innovations was known as DIANE, (Digital Integrated Attack and Navigation Equipment), which gave the flight crew the ability to pre-select multiple targets of opportunity both at night and in foul weather. The A-6 could, therefore, hit what its crew could not see. Its abilities made a particular impact on the North Vietnamese, who were astounded to discover

An A-6 Intruder (above) sat with its wings folded and its bomb pylons dangling empty, while the sun set on the *USS Saratoga* during Operation Desert Storm. The "Iron Tadpole," which first saw action in Vietnam, was in the twilight of its career.

that one of their power stations had been destroyed by only a pair of A-6s that had dropped 25 500-pound bombs—and not by a raid of B-52 bombers as they had originally thought.

The initial production run of 482 A-6As concluded in 1969. Later, 78 of these aircraft were converted into KA-6D tankers—a bizarre fate for an attack plane—with the addition of extra tanks, as well as a hose-drogue unit at the bottom of the fuselage, just forward of the tail.

The improved A-6E, which first flew in 1970, became considerably "smarter" in 1974, when a "target recognition attack multi-sensor" (TRAM) and a forward looking infrared system and laser designator/receiver were added. The A-6's reputation for evading enemy missiles was lionized in the Stephen Coonts military novel *Flight of the Intruder*. Then, in 1986, reality rubbed shoulders with fiction when the United States staged an attack against bases in Libya: Flying only tens of feet above the desert in complete darkness, A-6E Intruders eluded more than 100 anti-aircraft missiles and delivered their laser-guided weapons on target.

A-6Es continued to operate until early 1997, when the last unit, the "Sunday Punchers," was decommissioned. One hundred A-6Es that had previously been upgraded with composite wings were placed in "war reserve." The rest were stored for potential sale to friendly foreign governments.

VITALS	
Designation	A-6E Intruder
Wingspan	53 ft.
Length	54 ft. 9 in.
Max. Weight	58,600 pounds
Top Speed	644 mph
Cruising Speed	474 mph
Range	1010 miles (tactical)
Ceiling	42,400 ft.

Steam surged from a catapult on the *USS Independence* on Halloween 1996. The F-14 Tomcat (above) was wearing its usual costume: that of a fleet-defense, air-superiority supersonic fighter capable of carrying 13,000 pounds of snarling ordnance. The F-14 made its first kills in August 1981, when two Tomcats returned fire and shot down two Libyan Sukhoi Su-22 fighters over the Gulf of Sidra.

F-14
Tomcat

• Grumman

Immortalized in pop culture by the film "Top Gun," the F-14 Tomcat has permanently scratched its legacy into the annals of naval aviation.

The Grumman F-14 might have been more aptly named the Phoenix (which happens to be the name of one of its missiles) than the Tomcat. Like the legendary bird, the F-14 also rose from ashes, in this case the smoldering General Dynamic F-111B program, a failed attempt to build a one-size-fits-all fighter for the Air Force and Navy. The F-111A eventually found its way into the Air Force inventory; the Navy variant, the F-111B, proved to be too heavy for carrier operations and was cancelled. Faced with the pressing need to replace its aging F-4 Phantom IIs, the Navy was in a quandary. Grumman Aerospace Corp. had a possible contender to bridge the gap: Tom's Cat, as the F-14 would be nicknamed, in honor of its chief Pentagon proponent, Admiral Tom Collory. The F-14 had teething problems of its own, but it eventually became the Navy's most capable fighter.

VITALS

Designation	F-14 B/D Tomcat
Wingspan	38 ft. swept; 64 ft. unswept
Length	62 ft. 8 in.
Max. Weight	72,900 pounds
Top Speed	About 1240 mph
Cruising Speed	475 mph
Range	Over 1200 miles (tactical)
Ceiling	Above 50,000 ft.

The current versions of the Tomcat, the F-14B and F-14D, are supersonic, twin-engine, all-weather, multirole strike fighters. One of the most distinct features of the F-14 is that its entire airframe acts as a lifting body; less than half of the F-14's lift is created by its wings, which are notable for sweeping from 20 to 68 degrees automatically while in flight. On a carrier flight deck they can be withdrawn to a 75-degree over-swept position for parking. Fully extended, the wings span 64 ft., providing maximum lift for takeoff. However, this fully extended position creates fuel-robbing drag and is an impediment to high-performance maneuvering. As the plane gulps fuel and lightens in weight, its wings automatically sweep to a more efficient position.

The Tomcat's lethal cache of weapons is a mixed bag of up to 13,000 pounds of munitions. For air-to-air combat it can be equipped with Sparrow, Sidewinder and Phoenix missiles. For air-to-ground strikes, it can launch Harpoon antiship, HARM antiradar and Maverick antiarmor missiles. Droppable weapons include "dumb" or cluster bombs; specially equipped F-14s known as "Bombcats" can drop laser-guided bombs. And for unexpected close encounters, Tomcats protect themselves with a wing-mounted 20mm Vulcan cannon.

The F-14A/B models owe their weapons' high efficiency to a powerful Hughes AWG-9 pulse-Doppler radar, which can simultaneously track 24 targets while executing shooting solutions for any six. Aircrews flying the F-14D rely on an even more powerful and flexible radar, the AN/APG-71.

If the Tomcat's agile aerodynamics and intelligent avionics are its strength, its engines remain its weakness. The original F-14A was powered by a pair of Pratt & Whitney TF30 series turbofans, whose combined 41,800 pounds of thrust was barely sufficient for a fueled and armed aircraft that tipped the scales at almost 73,000 pounds. Additionally, the engines' turbine blades had an unfortunate tendency toward catastrophic failure. A simple warning light that alerted pilots to any sudden rise in engine breather pressure and impending engine disaster provided an inexpensive fix. Nevertheless, the Navy switched to more powerful General Electric F110-GE-400 turbofan engines when it replaced its F-14A with newer F-14B and F-14D versions. The combined 54,000 pounds of thrust from the General Electric engines overcame the power crunch, at lease initially. The loss of three of the re-engined aircraft

(continued)

The Grumman F-14 Tomcat (above) first took to the air in December 1970. All six of its nearly 1000-lb 13-ft. Phoenix missiles could be fired in rapid succession at six distinct targets, which could be identified at a distance of more than 130 miles. More than 630 of these long-range fighters were built for the U.S. Navy.

over a four-week period in 1996, however, led to temporary restrictions on the use of afterburners in all but emergency situations.

In the mid-1990s a digital flight-control system was introduced to prevent pilots from making maneuvers that were either unsafe or put undue stress on the airframe. Largely because of this effort, the Navy's projected 6000 flight-hour lifespan for the F-14 may be extended to as long as 9000 hours, making the Tomcat a formidable flying feline until 2010.

STEAM CATAPULT

As peppy as a Tomcat's General Electric turbofans may be, they're still not enough to accelerate a fully armed and loaded F-14 to takeoff speeds from an aircraft carrier. To safely launch from their floating hangars, modern naval combat planes need help from the catapult, a machine with roots in antiquity.

The steam catapult, invented by Britain's Royal Navy in 1951, consists of a pair of pointed-end pistons that race down a pair of cylinders. The piston's connector assembly manipulates a sealing strip of flexible metal that runs the length of the cylinders and seats against the cylinder's top-flange opening, allowing the steam pressure to be maintained; the connector also attaches to a shuttle that grasps the front wheel of the aircraft.

After the pilot signals his readiness with a smart salute, steam rushes into the cylinder behind the piston. When a restraining unit is released, the pistons shoot down the cylinders, taking the aircraft with them. The combined force of the steam catapult—enough power to propel a pickup truck more than two miles—and the thrust of the plane's engines on afterburners is sufficient to achieve takeoff speeds.

After the plane takes to the air, the pistons face the most traumatic part of their short journey. Their pointed tips run headlong into a pair of water-filled chambers, driving the pressure up and stopping the hard-working pistons in a space of less than 6 ft.

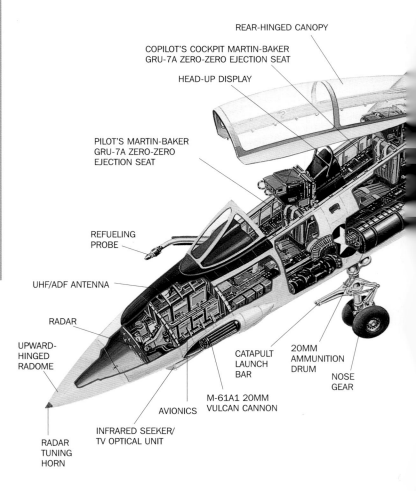

REAR-HINGED CANOPY

COPILOT'S COCKPIT MARTIN-BAKER GRU-7A ZERO-ZERO EJECTION SEAT

HEAD-UP DISPLAY

PILOT'S MARTIN-BAKER GRU-7A ZERO-ZERO EJECTION SEAT

REFUELING PROBE

UHF/ADF ANTENNA

RADAR

UPWARD-HINGED RADOME

RADAR TUNING HORN

AVIONICS

INFRARED SEEKER/ TV OPTICAL UNIT

M-61A1 20MM VULCAN CANNON

CATAPULT LAUNCH BAR

20MM AMMUNITION DRUM

NOSE GEAR

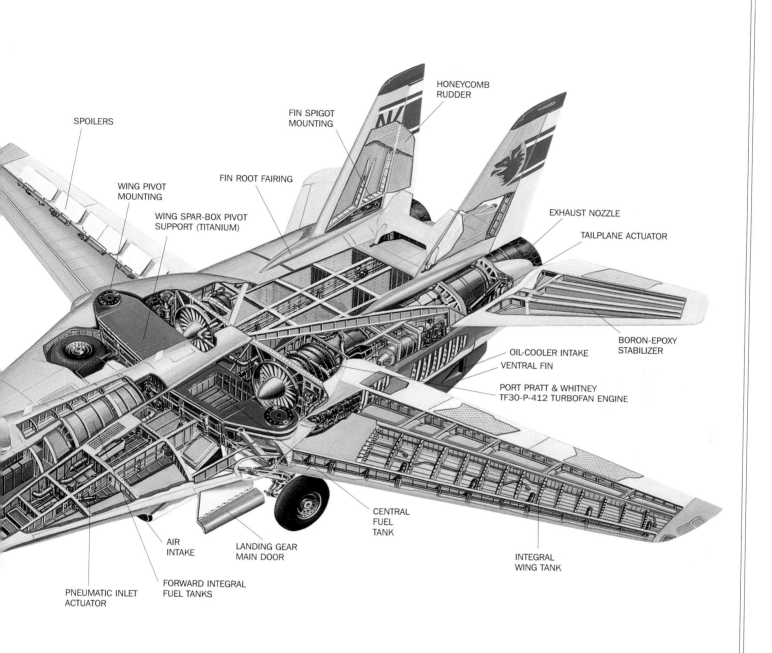

SPOILERS

WING PIVOT
MOUNTING

WING SPAR-BOX PIVOT
SUPPORT (TITANIUM)

FIN ROOT FAIRING

FIN SPIGOT
MOUNTING

HONEYCOMB
RUDDER

EXHAUST NOZZLE

TAILPLANE ACTUATOR

BORON-EPOXY
STABILIZER

OIL-COOLER INTAKE

VENTRAL FIN

PORT PRATT & WHITNEY
TF30-P-412 TURBOFAN ENGINE

PNEUMATIC INLET
ACTUATOR

AIR
INTAKE

FORWARD INTEGRAL
FUEL TANKS

LANDING GEAR
MAIN DOOR

CENTRAL
FUEL
TANK

INTEGRAL
WING TANK

F-14A Tomcat

The F/A-18 handily demonstrated its multipurpose capability during the first day of the Gulf War when two Hornets, en route to strike-mission targets, detected two Iraqi MiGs. The U.S. aircraft shot down both enemy planes and continued to their initial objective.

F/A-18
Hornet

• **McDonnell Douglas**

One of the sharpest stingers of Operation Desert Storm, the multimission F/A-18 flew nearly 9500 sorties against Iraqi forces.

Outside of television and movies, Americans get only fleeting glimpses of modern warplanes. The McDonnell Douglas F/A-18 Hornet is a proud exception. The Navy's most capable multimission plane is also the aircraft currently flown by the Blue Angels flight-demonstration squadron, whose heart-pounding aerobatic wizardry thrills thousands of people every year at air shows.

The Hornet's roots stretch back to the early

1970s, when the Pentagon decided that it needed smaller, less expensive aircraft to counter the improved fighters that the Soviet Union was selling to its allies. Initially, the Navy wanted separate F-18 fighter and A-18 attack aircraft, but in reaction to congressional pressure the projects were merged into what would become the F/A-18, the nation's first strike-fighter.

The basic Hornet airframe is derived from a

VITALS

Designation	F/A-18A/C Hornet
Wingspan	37 ft. 6 in.
Length	56 ft.
Gross Weight	Fighter 36,710 pounds; Attack 49,224 pounds
Top Speed	1190 mph
Cruising Speed	750 mph
Range	Fighter 460 miles (tactical); Attack 660 miles (tactical)
Ceiling	50,000 ft.

Northrop prototype that was originally designed for the U.S. Air Force but lost a competition against a General Dynamics plane that became the F-16 Fighting Falcon. The Navy, however, was interested in the Northrop design. Lacking aircraft-carrier expertise, Northrop teamed with McDonnell Douglas, which became the project's lead contractor.

Although the F/A-18 resembles the Northrop YF-17 at first glance, it is essentially a completely new airplane. To handle the trauma of catapult launches and arresting-wire landings, the new aircraft needed extensive modifications. The Navy's new plane paid for its strength with a slight dip in speed; its top speed clocked in at Mach 1.8 compared to the YF-17's Mach 2.0. The Hornet was blessed, however, with then state-of-the-art computer technology, which had been unavailable to the YF-17.

In November 1978, the Navy took delivery of the first of 11 developmental aircraft. Pilots were immediately surprised by both its speed and agility. In time, the crews that serviced the plane were also impressed by its reliability. Hornets have flown consistently without component failures for three times the hours of the Navy's other tactical aircraft, and they can be maintained in half the time.

The F/A-18A single seat and F/A-18B dual-seat Hornets proved so successful that the Navy ordered the F/A-18C Night Attack Hornet, which featured a pod-mounted Hughes AN/AAR-50 thermal-imaging navigation set and a forward-looking infrared radar-target-ing pod. Flown by a pilot wearing night-vision goggles, the F/A-18C became the ultimate night-attack aircraft. Another version, the F/A-18D two-seater, was adapted for reconnaissance. The F/A-18C and D also received improved navigation systems, including moving color maps and the ability to launch advanced, medium-range air-to-air missiles and Maverick infrared air-to-ground missiles.

The most recent addition to the family is the F/A-18E/F "Super Hornet." With a fuselage more than 4 ft. longer and a 25 percent larger wing area, it is a significantly larger aircraft than earlier Hornets, requiring two larger General Electric F414-GE-400 22,000-pound-thrust turbofans. Its predecessors use lower-power 16,000- and 17,700-pound-thrust General Electric F404-series engines.

As a weapons platform, the Hornet—rapidly configured as a fighter, attack aircraft or both—offers commanders unsurpassed flexibility. The F/A-18C/D can carry 13,700 pounds of externally mounted weapons, including wingtip-mounted Sidewinder missiles and numerous under-wing-mounted missiles. It can drop an assortment of weapons: "dumb," "smart" and nuclear.

This effective multimission aircraft has replaced the McDonnell F-4 Phantom II, the Douglas A-4 Skyhawk and the Grumman A-6 Intruder. In the years ahead, it promises to be even more useful, as it replaces the F-14 Tomcat and possibly the EA-6B Prowler electronic-warfare aircraft.

An F/A-18 Hornet (above) swept over azure waters toward a carrier deck in the final moments before landing. The Hornet's mission flexibility and relative cost-effectiveness has made it one of the most valuable warplanes in the U.S. military arsenal.

The SoloTrek XFV has yet to leave the ground. Bolstered, however, by a $5 million research grant, it is slated for testing by the U.S. Special Operations Command in mid-2003.

Three marines plummeted into free fall from a Bell-Boeing MV-22 Osprey (above) during a training exercise. The controversial Osprey tilt-rotor—23 marines lost their lives in two separate crashes in 2000—appears to have survived another tenuous period in its short history. As of June 2001, the DOD and the USMC indicated they favored restructuring rather than cancelling the Osprey program.

CHAPTER 9

The Future

Ambidextrous attack aircraft, exploding insects and lethal drones are now appearing in the crystal ball of combat aviation. What wondrous warplanes will be idling on the runway in the years to come?

In the first half of the 20th century, designing planes that could fly fast enough and far enough to succeed in combat posed the chief challenge to aeronautical engineers. By mid-century the jet engine had provided the definitive solution to both performance issues by removing the limitations on speed and reliability inherent in piston engines. Designers of military aircraft then turned their collective attention to increasing the survivability of combat aircraft and the destructive capacity of air-based weapons. Stand-off combat, fought with long-range radar and heat-seeking missiles, ren-

dered the dogfight obsolete, and the concept of airborne stealth—to attack an enemy without being seen or heard—became the new objective.

As the new century begins, the aviation industry finds itself on the verge of four separate transformations that will have as profound an impact on the future of combat planes as did the development of jet engines and stealth technology. The force propelling these innovations is the same as that which has revolutionized virtually every aspect of society it has touched: the computer.

The first of the four transformations is not

immediately obvious but is already in progress: the integration of computers into the combat aircraft itself. Automatic-pilot technology dates back decades, but true flight automation, which integrates both aircraft control and navigation, appeared for the first time in the F-117A Nighthawk fighter and the B-2 Spirit bomber. Both aircraft are too unstable to fly without the help of constant, subtle adjustments made by their on-board computers, which react faster than humans and can keep watch over many more flight parameters. This high degree of second-by-second control is also intrinsic to the design of the nation's next generation of warplanes. The Air Force F-22 air-superiority fighter; the multi-service Joint Strike Fighter (JSF) program—currently a hot competition between Boeing and Lockheed Martin prototypes—which will come in conventional, aircraft carrier-based and vertical-flight versions; and the Marine Corps MV-22 Osprey tilt-rotor, which is intended to replace troop-carrying helicopters, may all be radically different in their design and missions but share one essential design feature: Their computers are as vitally important to staying aloft as are their pilots.

But human fliers may not always be part of the equation. The inevitable next step, the development of pilotless aircraft, will bring about a second major transformation in military aviation. Unmanned Combat Aerial Vehicle (UCAV) research is being actively pursued by the U.S. Defense Advanced Research Projects Agency (DARPA), major aerospace companies and foreign governments. The immediate aim is to produce an aircraft with endurance capabilities beyond those of a piloted plane. By their basic design, UCAVs share more technology with cruise missiles than they do with airplanes. There is, however, one critical difference: A cruise missile reaches its target and explodes; a UCAV returns to its home base and lands.

Boeing's entry in the Joint Strike Fighter competition, the X-32 prototype (above) whizzed over Edwards AFB on its 17th test flight in November 2000. The future of the JSF program is somewhat murky due to budgetary and political uncertainties. The vertical-takeoff variant, which has the undivided attention of the U.S. Marine Corps, may have the best chance at receiving funding.

The idea of conducting aerial reconnaissance with a high-speed, high-altitude, unpiloted vehicle was an outgrowth of the CIA's Tagboard project, an effort mounted in the early 1960s in which an unmanned craft was to be launched from an A-12, the fraternal twin of the famous SR-71 high-speed spyplane. The program ended disastrously, with an A-12 crewman dead and his aircraft destroyed in a 1966 attempt to launch a D-21 drone at Mach 3.2.

The Northrop Grumman Global Hawk is the UCAV closest to becoming operational, having flown for the first time on February 28, 1998. The goal is to have it take off from bases in excess of 3000 miles from a battlefield and be able to "loiter" over its target area for as long as 24 hours. Flying at altitudes as high as 65,000 ft., it will gather intelligence by examining the battlefield

The main issue facing micro air vehicle (MAV) developers, (one moth-size version, inset) is a sufficiently lightweight powerplant. Far-flung applications for these killer bugs might include lethal reconnaissance MAVs that eliminate specific field commanders, after reading their iris patterns, and kamikaze titanium MAVs that get sucked into a jet engine's intakes, fracturing fan blades and spinning red-hot metal into the airframe.

simultaneously in visible light and at infrared frequencies, which reveal the telltale heat from engine exhaust. The Global Hawk will also be equipped with a moving-target indicator and synthetic-aperture radar, which will provide maps of unparalleled resolution and show the position and movement of ground forces. The Air Force has been pleased, thus far, with service tests.

The Boeing X-45A UCAV is on the verge of its first flight at NASA's Dryden Flight Test Center. High hopes have been pinned on this tailless, unmanned weapons platform, designed to knock out air defenses and conduct precision strikes.

The Lockheed Martin X-35 Joint Strike Fighter prototype (above) flies with a different version of the Pratt & Whitney JSF119 engine from the one propelling the competing Boeing X-32 prototype. The X-35's engine favors shaft power extraction over fan thrust and has the smaller fan of the two. Additionally, the X-35 has smaller dual inlets as opposed to the X-32's single 4-ft. inlet.

Current unmanned warplanes, derived largely from existing engine, avionics and weapons technologies, inhabit airframes that do not appear particularly "futuristic." This is, however, thought to be a temporary situation. Some experts believe that the computer brainpower that controls an F-22 will someday be reduced into a chip small enough to fit on the back of an aircraft about the size of a fly. By merging the aerodynamics of insects with ultra-small electronics, DARPA hopes to initiate the third transformation in combat flight, the creation of "micro air vehicles" (MAVs).

Too small to register on radar, MAVs would be able to "flap" their way into the most secret places on Earth and collect valuable intelligence. If these first spy-MAVs prove effective, the next generation would be modified to become armed and dangerous. Alan H. Epstein, professor of aeronautics and astronautics at the Massachusetts Institute of Technology, recently described one MAV combat scenario, in the technical journal *Aerospace America*. He envisions GPS-guided MAVs landing on structurally critical points along bridges deep in enemy territory. Each MAV would carry a small piece of shaped-charge plastique. Responding to a command transmitted from half a world away, the MAVs would explode in sequence, bringing down the bridge with only one-hundredth of the amount of explosives required by a pinpoint-accurate laser-guided smart bomb.

No matter how advanced MAVs become, there will always be a need for aircraft large enough to carry humans. But this doesn't necessarily mean that the aircraft that are the product of the fourth transformation will look anything like the human-carrying craft of today.

One of the most far-reaching proposals is a personal vertical-takeoff-and-landing aircraft. A California company, Millennium Jet Inc., has created a design that fuses a pair of ducted fan engines with a man-size exoskeleton-like structure. The exotic idea for the SoloTrek XFV has drawn both the interest of NASA and major development funding from DARPA. The vehicle would require minimal pilot training, be able to move individual special-forces troops as fast as 80 mph, remain airborne for an hour and a half and burn ordinary gasoline for fuel. Initial prototype tests are underway.

Aviation by computer, unmanned warplanes, aircraft the size of flies and a flying machine that you strap on your back may all seem like props from a science fiction movie. One hundred years ago, however, a similar assessment could have been made of the "impossible" machines proposed by Samuel Pierpont Langley, the Wright Brothers and the other aviation pioneers whose vision and tenacity lofted the great American warplanes.

The Boeing X-45A (above) was rolled out to meet the public in September 2000. The unmanned aircraft is 27 ft. long, weighs 8000 pounds and can carry 3000 pounds of weapons. A larger, more ambitious version for the Navy is currently in the pipeline. Naval planners envision a carrier-based drone that will carry more weapons, have a longer range and perform more surveillance duties.

The twin-engine Lockheed Martin F-22 Raptor is a state-of-the-art supersonic air-dominance fighter that combines agility with stealth technology; its prototype first flew on September 29, 1990. The Raptor is intended to replace the F-15 Eagle.

Index

Numerals in **boldface** indicate photographs.

A

A-4 Skyhawk, 79, **80,** 84, 183
A-6 Intruder, 157, **176,** 177, 183
A-7 Corsair II, 76, 80, **84,** 85, 86, 87
A-10 Thunderbolt, 73, 74-75, **80,** 81, **86, 87,** 88-89, **89**
A-11, 104
A-12, 104, 105, 187
A-17, 78
A-20 Havoc, 79, **82, 83,** 85
A-25 Helldiver, 169, 171
A-26 Invader, 79, 83
AC-47, 125, 180
AC-119, 125
AC-130 Spectre, 77, 80, 125
AH-1 Cobra, **136,** 142, **143,** 153, 173
AH-1J SeaCobra, 143
AH-1S HueyCobra, 144-145
AH-1T SeaCobra, **142**
AH-1W SuperCobra, 143, 145
AH-56 Cheyenne, 143
AH-64 Apache, **148, 149,** 150-151
Aircraft designation, 107
Apollo Lunar Excursion Module, 139
Arnold, General Henry H. "Hap," 22, 60
AV-8B Harrier, **90,** 91, 92-93

B

B1-B, **19**
B-1 Lancer, 29
B-2 Spirit, 19, **32, 33,** 34-35, 72, 80, 186
B-17 Flying Fortress, 15, 18, **20, 21,** 22-24, **26,** 58
B-24 Liberator, 16, 26, 58
B-26, 17, 79
B-29 Superfortress, 19, 24, **25,** 26, 128
B-36 Peacemaker, **26, 27,** 28
B-47 Stratojet, 15, 128
B-52 Stratofortress, 19, **28,** 30-31, 128, 177
B-57B Canberra, **18**
B-71, 104
Baghdad, 6
Baldwin Piano, 126
Béchereau, Louis, 45
Bell, Lawrence, 135
Bell Aircraft Corporation, 139, 148, 152
Bell Model 47, 135, 137, 139
Berliner, Emile, 135
Berliner, Henry, 135
Birkigt, Marc, 45
Boeing 247, 21
Boeing 707-320B, 108, 109, 111
Boeing Company, 18, 20, 152, 186
Bong, Richard, 48, 61
Breguet, Louis, 135

C

C-2 Greyhound, 118, **156**
C-2A, 128
C-5 Galaxy, 120, 147
C-17 Globemaster III, **117,** 118, **152**
C-47 Skytrain, 118, 121, **122, 123,** 124-125, 127, 146
C-53 Skytrooper, 122
C-54 Skymaster, 125
C-119, 119
C-130 Hercules, 114-115, 118, 147
C-135, 107
C-141 Starlifter, 120
Campbell, Steve, 29
Carter, Jimmy, 29
CG-2A Haig (Hadrian), 121, **126, 127**
CG-4A, 123
CH-34, 173
CH-46 Sea Knight, **172, 173**
CH-47 Chinook, 133, **140, 141,**
CH-60 Seahawk, 147
Consolidated Aircraft Corporation, 27
Cornu, Paul, 135
Curtiss Aircraft, 158
Curtiss Hawk, 53
CV-4, 158

D

D-21, 187
Da Vinci, Leonardo, 134
De Bothezat, George, 133, 135
De Havilland DH-4, 44
DC-3, 122, 125
DC-10, 118, 129
Douglas Aircraft Company, 21, 24, 85

E

E-3 Sentry, 100, **108, 109**
E-4 National Airborne Operations Center, 94-95, 100, **110, 111,** 112-113
EA-6B Prowler, **157,** 176, 183
Edison, Thomas Alva, 135
Eisenhower, Dwight D., 102, 118
Ejection seats, 71
Ely, Eugene, 158
Enola Gay, 25
EP-3 ARIES II, **160**
Epstein, Alan H., 188

F

F-4 Phantom II, 43, **64,** 65, 66, 67, 101, 178, 183
F4U Corsair, **166, 167**
F-8 Crusader, 85
F9C-2 Sparrowhawk, **158**
F-14 Tomcat, **154-155, 178, 179,** 180-181
F-15 Eagle, **66,** 69, 73
F-16 Fighting Falcon, 42, **68, 69,** 70, 71, 73, 183
F-22 Raptor, 42, 67, 80, 186, 188, **189**
F-47, **54**
F-80 Shooting Star, 60, **61,** 66
F-86 Sabre, **62, 63**
F-94 Starfire, 61
F-104 Starfighters, 41
F-111A, 178
F-111B, 178
F-117 Nighthawk, **6,** 32, 42, **72,** 73, 186
F/A-18 Hornet, 73, **182, 183**

F

Fat Man (atomic bomb), 25
Federation of American Scientists, 67
Ficker, Jacob E, 77
Flying Tigers, 40
Focke-Wulf, 20
Fokker, Anthony, 40
Fokker Aircraft, 40
Ford Motor Company, 126
Fort Sam Houston, 8
Fw-190, 20

G

General Dynamics, 68, 104
Global Hawk, 187
Göring, Hermann, 40, 58
Great Aerodrome, **8, 9,** 10
Groom Dry Lake Bed, Nevada, 73
Grumman Aircraft Corporation, 85
Guam, 33

H

H-1, 133, 135
H-12, 156
H-13, 136, **138, 139,** 140, 141
HH-60 Rescue Hawk, 133
HH-60G Night Hawk, 147
Harrier GR.1, 91
Hawker P.1127, 91
Hawker-Sidley, 91
Hiroshima, Japan, 19
Hispano-Suiza, 45
Holland, John, 160
HTL-1, 139
HTL-4, 139
Hughes Aircraft Company, 148, 149

I

Il'ya Muromets, 17
Inman, Chris, 33

J

Johnson, Clarence "Kelly," 51, 60, 102
Joint Strike Fighter, 80, 186, 187

K

KA-6D, 177
Kartveli, Alexander, 54
KC-10 Extender, 118, **128,** 129
KC-135, 105, 129
Kitty Hawk, North Carolina, 6, 8, 26

L

L2D3, 122
Laddon, Isaac Maclin, 162
Lambert, Lawrence, 71
Langley, Samuel Pierpont, 8, 9, 10, 188
Lavochkin, 61
LeMay, General Curtis E., 25
Li-2, 122
Liberty Plane (DH-4), **10**

Lindbergh, Charles, 158
Little Boy (atomic bomb), 25
Lockheed Aircraft Company, 21, 24, 49, 60, 68, 102, 104, 186
Luzon, Philippines, 52

M

McDonnell Aircraft Corporation, 64
McDonnell Douglas Corporation, 91, 149, 152
McGuire, Tommy, 48
McKinley, William, 9Manley, Charles M., 9, 10
Mariana Islands, 25
MASH units, 136
Me 62, 61
Me 109, 53
Me 262, 62
Messerschmitt, 56
MH-47E, 141
MH-60 Pave Hawk, 147
Micro air vehicle (MAV), **187,** 188
MiG-15, 61, 62, 63, 66
MiG-23, 66
MiG-25, 66
Millennium Jet, Inc., 188
Mitchell, General William "Billy," 141
Mitchell Field, 50
Mitsubishi A6M Zero-Sen, 53
Model 7B (Douglas), 82
Model 107 (Vertol), 173
Model 299 (Boeing), 21
Moulton, Steve, 33
Musashi (Japanese carrier), 169
Mutual Assured Destruction (MAD), 19
MV-22 Osprey, **185,** 186

N

Nagasaki, Japan, 19
NC-4, 158
Norden, Carl, 23
North American Aviation, 56, 57, 62, 85
Northrop, 68

O

O-52 Owl, 99
OH-58 Kiowa, **135,** 153
Oliver, Mike, 29

P

P-3 Orion, 97
P-3M, 162
P-12, 39
P-26 Peashooter, **39**
P-36, 53
P-38 Lightning, 41, **48, 49,** 50-51, 52, 53, 59, 62
P-40 Warhawk, 40, 49, **52, 53,** 56, **146**
P-47 Thunderbolt, 42, 54, **55,** 58, 68
P-51 Mustang, 52, 53, **56, 57,** 58-59, 171
P-59 Airacomet, 62
P-61 Black Widow, 83
P-70, 83
P-80 Shooting Star, **60,** 61
P-86 Sabre, 62

Paul E. Garber Restoration and Storage Facility, 133
PBY Black Cats, 163
PBY Catalina, **162, 163,** 164-165
Pearl Harbor, 52, 53
Potomac River, 9
Powers, Francis Gary, 96
Pratt & Whitney, 55

R

R4D, 122
RAH-66 Comanche, **134,** 152, **153**
RC-135, 107
Republic Aviation, 54
RF-4C, **100**
Richet, Charles, 135
Rickenbacker, Eddie, 45, 46
Roosevelt, Theodore, 8
RS-71, 104
Ryan Aircraft, 91

S

S-2C Tracker, **159**
S-3A Viking, **161**
SB2C Helldiver, **168, 169**
SBD Dauntless, 168
SC.1, 90, 91
Schmued, Edgar, 56
Short Brothers, 90
Sikorsky, Igor, 17, 135
Sikorsky Aircraft, 152
Skunk Works, 51, 60, 73
Smithsonian Institution, 9
Société pour l'Aviation et ses Dérives (SPAD), 44
Solotrek XFV, **184,** 188
Sopwith Camel, 40
SPAD XIII, 40, **44, 45,** 46-47
SR-71 Blackbird, **98,** 100, 103, **104, 105,** 106-107, 187
Su-22, 178
Su-35, 67
Su-37, 67

T

T-33, 61
Tibbets, Colonel Paul, 24, 25

U

U-2 Dragon Lady, **96,** 100, **102, 103,** 104
UH-1 Iroquois, **137,** 142, 146, 147
UH-60 Black Hawk, **146, 147**
UH-60Q, 146
Unmanned Combat Aerial Vehicle (UCAV), 186, 187
USS Abraham Lincoln, 175-176, **176**
USS Bunker Hill, 168
USS Dwight D. Eisenhower, 76
USS Independence, **178**
USS John F. Kennedy, 84, **154-155**
USS Leyte, **167**

V

V-22 Osprey, 136, 173
V-144, 140
Van Richthofen, Manfred, 40
Verne, Jules, 160
VH-60N White Hawk, 147
Vought Aircraft Company, 84, 85

W

Waco Aircraft Company, 126
Ward Furniture, 126
Widewater, Virginia, 9
Whiteman Air Force Base, 33
Williams, Richard L., 21
Wright Brothers, 6, 8, 17, 135
Wright Military Flyer, 6, **7,** 8, 77, 96, 135, 188
Wright-Patterson Air Force Base, 133

X

X-13, 91
X-32, **186** (see also Joint Strike Fighter)
X-35, **187** (see also Joint Strike Fighter)
X-45A, **188**
XB-47, **14**

Y

Yak, 61
Yalu River, 61
Yamamoto, Admiral Isoruku, 164
Yamato (Japanese carrier), 169
Yeager, Charles "Chuck," 46
YF-12A, 104
YF-17, 183
Young, Arthur, 135, 139
YR-13, 138
YR-13A, 139

Z

Zeppelin, 77

Photo Credits

Sources

BOOKS

Ambrose, Stephen E. *D-Day June 6, 1944: The Climactic Battle of World War II*. New York: Simon & Shuster, 1994.

Angelucci, Enzo. *The American Fighter*. New York: Orion Books, 1985.

Bonds, Ray, ed, *The U.S. War Machine*. New York: Crown, 1978.

Crickmore, Paul F. *Lockheed SR-71: The Secret Missions Exposed*. Osceola, Wis.: Motorbooks International, 1997.

Davis, Larry. *Planes, Names & Dames Vol. I 1940-1945*. Carrollton, Texas: Squadron/Signal Publications, 1990.

Donald, David, and Jon Lake, eds. *The Encyclopedia of World Military Aircraft*. New York: Barnes & Noble/Aerospace Publishing, 2000.

Frawley, Gerard. *The International Directory of Military Aircraft*. Fyshwick, Australia: Aerospace Publications, 2000.

Gunston, Bill. *History of Military Aviation*. London: Hamlyn, 2000.

Keegan, John. *The Second World War*. New York: Penguin Books, 1990.

Lee, David. *Boeing: From Peashooter to Jumbo*. Edison, N.J.: Chartwell Books, 1999.

Lightbody, Andy, and Joe Payer. *The Illustrated History of Helicopters*. Lincolnwood, Ill.: Publications International, 1990.

McFarland, Stephen L. *A Concise History of the U.S. Air Force*. Washington, D.C.: Air Force History and Museums Program, 1997.

————. *America's Pursuit of Precision Bombing, 1910-1945*. Washington, D.C.: Smithsonian Institution, 1995.

Mondey, David, and Michael Taylor. *The Guinness Book of Aircraft Record Facts and Feats*. New York: Canopy Books, 1992.

Ness, William H., Frederick A. Johnsen, and Chester Marshall. *Big Bombers of WWII*. Ann Arbor, Mich.: Lowe & B. Hould Publishers, 1998.

Shul, Brian. *Sled Driver: Flying the World's Fastest Jet*. Chico, Calif.: MACH 1, 1991.

Wagner, Ray. *American Combat Planes*. Garden City, N.Y.: Doubleday, 1982.

Young, Warren: *The Helicopters*. Alexandria, Va.: Time-Life Books, 1982.

Zich, Arthur. *World War II: The Rising Sun*. Alexandria, Va.: Time-Life Books, 1977.

PERIODICALS AND ARTICLES

Aboulafia, Richard. "Rethinking U.S. Air Power." *Aerospace America*, Mar. 2001.

"Airship Proves A Good Submarine." *Popular Mechanics*, Nov. 1903.

Anderson, Jon R. "Apaches Are Ailing Warriors." *Stars and Stripes*, Dec. 19, 2000.

Cordesman, Anthony H. "The Lessons … Missile Campaign in Kosovo." Center for Strategic Assessment, Washington, D.C.

Eckland, K.O. "The Wright Brothers." (www.aerofiles.com/bio_w.html#wright).

Ford, Daniel. "B-36." *Air & Space*, Apr./May 1996.

Glines, C.V. "The Flying Octopus." *Air Force Magazine*, Oct. 1990.

Knott, Richard. "U.S. Naval Aviation at 90." (www.aviationnow.com/content/ncof/ncf_n17.htm).

Lishman, Gordon, "Evolution of Helicopter Flight." (www.flight100.org/history/helicopter.html).

"Oxcart Story, The." *Air Force Magazine*, Nov. 1994.

Sidley, Hugh. "D-Day, The Home Front." *Time* domestic online edition, Jun. 13, 1994.

Vivian, E. Charles. "History of Aeronautics." (www.bookrags.com/books/haero/PART11.htm).

WEB SITES

www.acala1.ria.army.mil; www.af.mil/news/factsheets; www.armyavmuseum.org; www.aviation.army.mil; www.aviation-history.com; www.boeing.com; www.britannica.com; www.chinfo.navy.mil; www.edwards.af.mil; www.fas.org; www.history.navy.mil; www.nasm.edu; www.naval-air.org; www.northgrum.com; www.sikorsky.com; www.solotrek.com; www.voughtaircraft.com; www.warbirddalley.com; www.warbirdsresourcegroup.org; www.wpafb.af.mil.